HUNTER'S FLEET

Percy Hunter looking out over the Yard that he founded with his sons Cyril and Stanley.

Hunter's Fleet

Richard Johnstone-Bryden

Foreword by Lady Ralphs

Nighthawk Publishing
Halesworth, United Kingdom

First published in 2004 by
Nighthawk Publishing - Halesworth - Suffolk - IP19OHG

British Library Cataloguing in Publication Data
A catalogue record for this book is available from the British Library

ISBN   1-84280-073-6

Origination and electronic formating in .PDF by
Nighthawk Publishing

Printed by Micropress Halesworth Suffolk
(info@micropress.co.uk)

By the same Author

Published books

Britain's Greatest Warship — HMS Ark Royal (IV)
(Sutton Publishing)

The Royal Yacht Britannia — The Official History
(Conway Maritime Press)

Norfolk Wherries
(Nighthawk Publishing)

Forthcoming books

History of the Fleet Air Arm in the Twentieth Century
(Fleet Air Arm Museum)

Boats To Build
(Nighthawk Publishing)

MTB 102 - Dunkirk Flagship
(Nighthawk Publishing)

Wood Avens in the River Thurne.

Contents

Author's Note		9
Acknowledgements		11
Foreword	by Lady Ralphs	13
Chapter One	A Unique Yachting Environment	15
Chapter Two	A Leap Of Faith	43
Colour Plates	I to VIII	after 64
Chapter Three	The County's Fleet	73
Colour Plates	IX to XVI	after 96
Chapter Four	The Bombshell	101
Appendix I	The Details	131
Appendix II	Notable Events	141
Appendix III	The Trustees	145
Appendix IV	Slipping The Yachts	147
Glossary		155
Bibliography		157
Index		158

Hunter's Yard.

Author's Note

Through my work as a marine writer and photographer I have followed the story of Hunter's Fleet since 1995. My first contact with the Yard was thanks to the Editor of the magazine The Boatman, Pete Greenfield, who rang me in January 1995 to invite me to produce an article about the Fleet for publication later in the year. Within a few weeks of accepting this commission the story became much bigger than either of us could have imagined thanks to Norfolk County Council's controversial decision to sell the Fleet. I, like so many others, watched with interest as the struggle to save the Fleet got underway that Spring with various organisations expressing interest in acquiring this unique fleet. Thankfully, the Fleet avoided the real threat of being modernised or dispersed and those interested in preserving the Fleet for future generations came together to form the Norfolk Heritage Fleet Trust.

Since then I have maintained my links with the Yard by covering the restoration of *Rebel Reveller*, *Woodcut* and the construction of the new 4 berth yacht as well as taking photographs for the annual brochure. During the course of these visits the idea of producing a book to record the rich and varied history of the Fleet was discussed from time to time but remained nothing more than an aspiration, until the beginning of 2003 when I was commissioned by the Trust to write this book.

The objective of this book was to set down the full story of Hunter's Fleet for the first time and provide the background to the key events within the Fleet's history. As with any historical work the research for this book has been a mixture of excitement and extreme frustration. During the course of the project I have come across many items that challenge the previously accepted chronology for the Fleet. Equally, some of the surviving documentation failed to provide conclusive answers to a number of important questions that may never be solved because the only people who could help are no longer with us. However, one important factor began to emerge throughout the history of the Fleet and that was the part played by good luck - without it there would be no story to tell.

Richard Johnstone-Bryden
Suffolk
January 2004

Acknowledgements

During the course of the research for this book I have received a great deal of help from various people who have either given up their time to tell me about their memories of the Fleet or lent me documents and photographs. I would like to take this opportunity to draw people's attention to the wonderful new archive facilities that we now have in Norwich. I have been fortunate enough to rely on records held by both the Norfolk Heritage Centre in the Forum and the Norfolk Record Office in County Hall.

I would like to begin by thanking Lady Ralphs for agreeing to write the foreword to this history and for contributing directly to the text.

I would especially like to thank the following people and organisations, listed in alphabetical order:

Mrs Lesley Bonshor,
Mr Ron Bonshor,
Mr Neil Bowles, Class Captain, Waveney One Design Class,
Professor Keith Clayton CBE
Mr Graham Cooper,
Eastern Daily Press,
Mrs Heather Evans, Secretary, Yare & Bure One Design Class,
Mr Kingsley Farrington, Official Builder of the Yare & Bure One Design,
Mrs Jean Gee,
Mr Les Gee,
Mr Ian Grapes,
Mr Tom Grapes,
Mr David Hastings MBE,
Mr Peter Hollingham
Mr Bill Housden, The Broads Authority,
Mr Alex Humphris, The Rebel One Design Class,
Mr Michael Hunter, Jeckells of Wroxham Ltd,
Mr Geoff Keighley,
The Rev Neville Khambatta,
Liz Mace,
Mrs Jennifer Mack,
Mrs Lisa Morgan,
The Norfolk Record Office,

Mr G.L. Oakenfold,
Mr Bryan Read CBE DL,
Mr Jim Searle,
Mrs Jill Searle,
Mr Tim Shaw, Democratic Services Norfolk County Council,
Mr Michael Sparks, The Norfolk Wherry Trust,
Mr Paul Stevens,
Mr Rodney Storey,
Mrs Christine Taylor,
Mr Geoff Thompson,
Mrs Josie Webb,
Mr Clive Wilkins-Jones,
The Norfolk Heritage Centre,
The Forum, Norfolk & Norwich Millennium Library,
Mr Simon Whipp
Mrs E.M. Witton,
Mr Richard Young,

To turn my work into a printed bound volume, some advanced processes were employed. These enabled me to participate in the stages of production to the point where the printing presses took over. In addition to reducing production costs, it enabled me to retain influence to the end of the process, which is not normally an opportunity afforded to an author. I would therefore offer a special thanks to Nighthawk Publishing for producing the electronic master, and to the FIRE Project development team who created the technology and techniques employed to produce the master. Finally, I would like to thank Micropress for their assistance in copying the electronic master into the computer-controlled press that printed the book.

Foreword

The Broads and their connecting rivers are an area of unique beauty and amenities. Once an artery of commerce they have become a centre of recreation. This book is the inspiring story of sailing enthusiasts anxious to share the modern day skill and fun of their ancient craft while remaining responsible custodians of the natural environment and trustees for its future.

It all began when one man shared his vision with his sons. All three pooled their skills. With grim determination to succeed they built the boats and evolved the boat yard. It became a centre of excellence which still challenges successors to maintain the "Hunter standard". Then as always it gave a life enhancing experience to hundreds of hirers who often made sailing a family affair, an experience passed on from one generation to the next.

Norfolk school children were fortunate in that when Hunter's Yard closed The Norfolk County Sailing Base opened. Insightful educationalists realised that education extends beyond the classroom and that children learn much by doing. Sailing taught skills and showed that discipline is not necessarily something imposed by adults but arises from circumstances. Self discipline is essential in acquiring the art of sailing and brings its own life long reward. Sailing teaches how much it matters to others how we behave and that we can make the difference between safety and disaster. Much in the art of sailing is caught as well as taught. Youngsters owe an immense debt of gratitude to dedicated teachers, enthusiasts themselves, who were unstinting of their time, imparted their skills and shared fellowship and fun with their pupils. Sometime the process began before a keel touched water. Woodwork teachers assisted pupils to build Bitterns. When called upon to launch them, I could not but realise their importance in giving young people an insight into the significance of integrity in workmanship, vital to the well being of others as well as of themselves.

All might have been lost but for the vision of the trustees who founded The Norfolk Heritage Fleet Trust. It is an enterprise for young and old which remains faithful to its undertaking to keep "education in its widest sense as its main aim", to maintain "the necessary boat building skills needed to build and maintain wooden yachts", and to provide the much appreciated preferential rate for the educational use of the boats by Norfolk schools and the Norfolk Youth and Community Service. Lower rates are also available to youth groups from outside the county. Womack Waters still echo with the voices of teachers and taught as they embark with excitement and return with satisfaction, more than a little tinged with regret at the end of a perfect experience.

It required great public spirit, foresight and courage to set up the Trust. The result is a well run yard with trustees and staff who are realistic about good times and undaunted by difficulties and tight schedules. Generations are learning what it means to be shipmates and many are the reminiscences of the Broads and their rivers which are at once unique and universal.

The author has given us an invaluable and painstaking history of three phases in the life of the yard recorded while it is still possible to contact many of the participants. Long may the enterprise he portrays continue to make its outstanding contribution to the vitality of a well loved region.

Lady Ralphs
Norfolk, February 2004

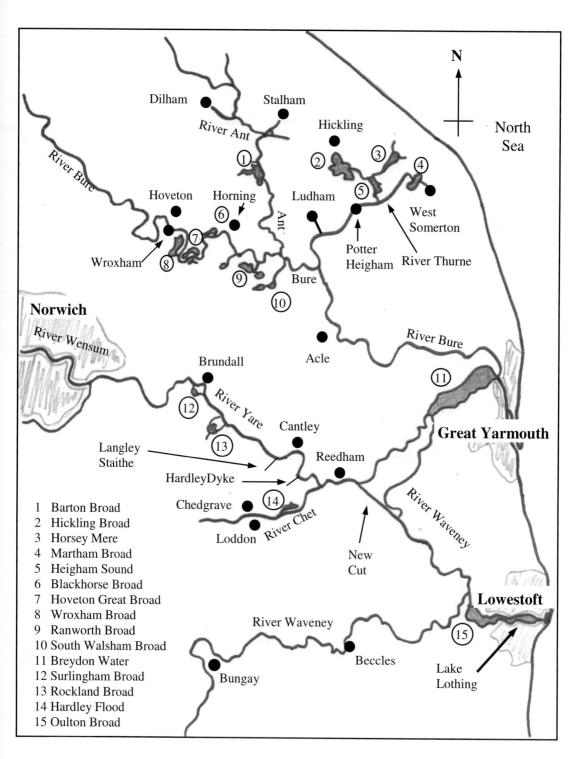

Above: A sketch of the navigable rivers and Broads indicating the main geographical features of the area. ©Seaquest Associates

The Broads are teaming with wildlife, such as this heron seen on the banks of the River Bure. © Richard Johnstone-Bryden

Chapter One
A Unique Yachting Environment
A Guide To The Norfolk & Suffolk Broads

The Norfolk and Suffolk Broads are home to the yachts and half deckers that make up Hunter's Fleet. This unique sailing environment is often overlooked when people try to examine the reasons behind the long term appeal of Hunter's Fleet. Although much has changed on the Broads since the Hunter family established their yard at Ludham the basic magic remains the same and continues to attract generation after generation of holiday makers who come to experience the thrill of Broadland sailing.

So what are the Broads like? The 125 miles of navigable waters consist of rivers and lakes (known as Broads). Despite their idyllic appearance,

The Broads are home to over 900 indigenous classic sailing craft, such as these Broads yachts of the River Cruiser Class.

© Richard Johnstone-Bryden

the various Broads were in fact Medieval peat diggings that subsequently flooded to become an attractive part of the Broadland environment. Each of these Broads provides a refreshing change from river sailing, with reasonable sized expanses of open water. They act as an ideal venue, either for some exciting uninterrupted sailing, or to simply drop the mud weight over the bow and watch the world go by. Alternatively, they are a safe place, for those new to sailing, to learn the basics before trying the more challenging conditions of the rivers.

The Broadland network is essentially split into two "zones" linked by a 4 mile stretch of open water known as Breydon Water. In Roman times Breydon Water was a vast open estuary that became progressively smaller as it silted up. For many first time visitors to the Broads, their biggest challenge is a crossing over Breydon Water. The channel is clearly marked by navigation posts and you should keep within these markers AT ALL TIMES because it is quite shallow outside the channel and often dries out at low water. When sailing on Breydon Water it is important to make sure that you do not catch either your topping lift, or mainsheet, on one of the navigation posts, because there is a good chance you could lose your mast! Crossing Breydon Water is usually straightforward but it can get relatively choppy, with short steep waves, when there is a strong wind against tide.

Picture postcard locations, such as the village of Horning with its pretty thatched cottages, have attracted generations of holiday makers to the Broads. © Richard Johnstone-Bryden

The Northern Rivers

Hunter's Yard is located within the Northern "zone" which is blessed with more Broads, and made up of the Rivers Bure, Thurne and Ant. It was on these rivers that the Broadland tourism industry was pioneered by a mixture of enterprising wherry and boatyard owners, who saw the opportunity to profit from the interest created by the wealth of magazine articles and books published about the Broads during the second half of the 19th Century. This relationship has resulted in the Northern "zone" becoming the best known part of the Broads, with picture postcard locations, such as the village of Horning and Horsey Mere, being used to attract generations of holiday makers to the area.

Broadland sailing holidays reached their peak in the 1930s with a wide selection of boats available for hire, from the mighty wherry yachts, of about 60ft, through to half deckers, and dinghies. The outbreak of the Second World War brought an abrupt halt to the whole industry, as the Government restricted access to the rivers, and seized as many craft as possible to moor on open stretches to prevent German seaplanes from landing. When peace returned, the hire indus-

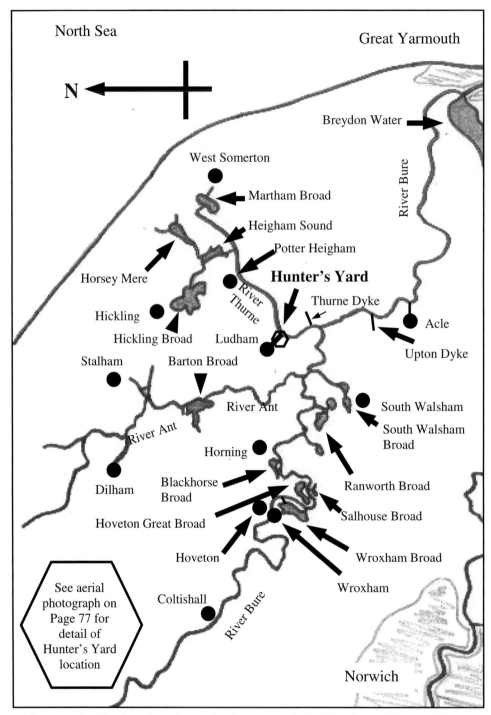

Above: Sketch showing the main features of the Northern Rivers. The access to the Southern Rivers via Great Yarmouth to Breydon Water is marred by the low air draft under the Bure bridges at Great Yarmouth.

© Seaquest Associates

Wiseman's Mill, Oby. © Richard Johnstone-Bryden

try initially resumed around sailing craft, because petrol rationing prevented the use of motor cruisers. With the lifting of fuel restrictions, the number of motor cruisers began to steadily increase during the 1950s and 1960s as they took the place of many sailing craft in hire fleets throughout the Broads. Having reached their peak in the late 1970s the numbers of hire craft on the Broads have steadily dropped as many of those who once hired motor cruisers have since opted for cheaper holidays abroad. Interestingly, the decline of the main hire fleet industry has coincided with a revival of the Broadland sailing holiday with a small number of specialist boatyards building and restoring classic Broadland sailing craft for hire.

The River Bure

The Northern "zone" is not accessible to yachts with fixed masts, because the entrance to the River Bure, from the North Sea port of Great Yarmouth, is spanned by the Vauxhall Bridge and the A47 Road Bridge. The lower of the two bridges can only be used by boats with an air draft of less than 6ft 9in at average high water. However, both bridges do have a gauge that indicates the available air draft so, if you time your passage to coincide with low water, you could gain an extra few feet clearance at the expense of depth. As you approach or leave Great Yarmouth do not forget that the rivers are tidal. This might be stating the obvious but many first time visitors to the Broads do not appreciate this fact and it comes as an unpleasant surprise. As a rule, the closer you get to Great Yarmouth, the stronger the tides. Like the other rivers of the Broads, the River Bure is covered by a set of speed limits, ranging from 6mph down to 3mph, that are clearly marked by signs along the river bank and apply to all powered craft. These limits are rigorously enforced, and breaking them could result in a significant fine.

Before you reach Great Yarmouth Yacht Station, it is a good idea to carefully consider your plans because they are the only safe moorings between the entrance to the Bure and The Stracey Arms, which is approximately 8 miles, and at least 1.5 hours away under power. When navigating the lower reaches of the Bure it is important not to get too close to the insides of bends, especially on a falling tide, because many of them have become increasingly shallow as a result of silting up. Some of the worst bends have painted stakes clearly marking the extent of projecting mud banks. The river between Great Yarmouth and Stracey Arms runs through open marshland and can feel very empty at times, particularly in the winter months when there are very few boats out on the water. As you leave the hustle and bustle of Great Yarmouth behind you, the only landmarks on the horizon are a series of derelict wind pumps in varying degrees of neglect.

Just when you feel as though you have escaped civilisation, the distinctive profile of Stracey Mill looms into sight. The preserved mill, managed by the Norfolk Windmill Trust, is open to visitors during the summer season. Next to the mill there are good moorings and a pub. Alternatively, if you keep going, there is the small country pub at Stokesby which was once one of the five places around the Broads to operate a chain ferry. By Acle bridge there is a good pub and a small shop selling provisions. For those needing to drop their mast there are good moorings either side of the bridge. The reed-lined river, between Acle bridge and Thurne Mouth, offers some of the best river sailing to be found within the Northern "zone" with reasona-

Thurne Mouth becomes extremely congested during the annual regatta, as competitors jostle for position.   © Richard Johnstone-Bryden

bly long wide open stretches of river. This area is also a popular place with anglers and you will see a number of small stagings that are for fishermen only and not to be used for mooring. In an attempt to reduce the tensions between yachtsmen and anglers a fishing zone was created along this part of the river

Former hire fleet motor cruiser *Juliette* makes her way down Candle Dyke.
© Richard Johnstone-Bryden

that yachtsmen are asked to avoid using before 0900 on a Sunday morning. Upton Dyke is perhaps the best place to stop along this part of the Bure. At the end of the narrow dyke there are good moorings and a free slipway for dinghies. The village of Upton is about a mile away and has a post office, shop and the White Horse pub.

The River Thurne

As you emerge from Upton Dyke, to rejoin the Bure, the two mills that mark Thurne Mouth are soon visible. The point at which the River Thurne flows into the Bure can often feel like a motorway junction at the height of the summer season, with boats converging on this stretch of water from either Potter Heigham, Horning, or Great Yarmouth. Great caution should be exercised as you pick your way through the various hire craft, many of which are being driven by people who have never handled a boat before and know very little about what they are doing, or about the rules of the 'road'. Whilst it might be very satisfying to simply shout at these boats if they get in the way you can avoid most problems by giving clear hand signals indicating which side you want them to pass you on if you are tacking up a river and when you want them to pass. Don't forget they are also on holiday trying to have fun, so a bit of positive guidance can avoid stressful situations!

For those sailing up from Acle bridge, their good sailing is likely to continue for most of the way up to the outskirts of Potter Heigham. The only disruption to the open marshland is caused by the trees near Thurne Dyke and by the entrance to Womack Water. Thurne Dyke has plenty of moorings and there are public toilets, telephone, post box, a small shop, and a pub close to the staithe. Alternatively, you could keep going and pay a visit to Hunter's Yard. For those who want to visit the pretty village of Ludham there are public moorings at Womack Staithe. The village itself is only a short walk away and boasts a pub, village store, and a post office. On rejoining the Thurne you will find the reed-lined banks soon give way to the various riverside bungalows of Potter Heigham. The large yacht marina built by Herbert Woods close to the bridge was probably the first marina of its type to be built when it was completed in 1931. The 2 acre basin was literally dug out by hand to provide 1800ft of quay heading for his hire fleet of motor cruisers and yachts. On the opposite side of the river lies the pilot station operated by Robin and Patrick Richardson. Most hire boats must be taken through the bridge by a pilot and those unfamiliar with the notorious medieval bridge would be well advised to use their services. There are good public moorings either side of the two road bridges at Potter Heigham (Medieval bridge 6.75ft air draft & 7.75ft air draft for the "new" bypass bridge). The village has a post office, Lathams general store, a small games arcade, and perhaps the best fish and chip shop on the Broads

The ruins of St. Benets Abbey. © Richard Johnstone-Bryden

Soon after leaving Potter Heigham on the opposite bank to Candle Dyke lies the river frontage of Martham Boatbuilding & Development Co. The yard was founded in 1946 by Jimmy Brown and subsequently went on to become the third largest boatyard on the Broads. There is another of the Broads Authority fishing zones upriver of Martham Ferry that yachtsmen are asked to avoid before 0900 on a Sunday morning. This relatively narrow reed-lined piece of river eventually opens up to reveal Martham Broad, although you must keep to the main channel. The river terminates at West Somerton's public staithe that has some good public moorings. Perhaps the most striking aspect of West Somerton is that the water is so clear, you can actually see the river bed!

Instead of heading towards West Somerton at Martham, you could sail up the entrance to Candle Dyke, which leads to Hickling Broad and Horsey Mere. The channel through Heigham Sound is clearly marked and you should keep to it at all times, because it is quite shallow outside the channel. Despite the expanse of open water the same applies as you sail on Hickling Broad. At the top of Hickling Broad there are moorings by the Pleasure Boat pub. Alternatively, at the top of Heigham Sound, you could sail up the relatively narrow Meadow Dyke to Horsey Mere, which offers better sailing for yachts than Hickling Broad. The only moorings at

The mouth of the River Ant. © Richard Johnstone-Bryden

Horsey Mere are at the end of the staithe where a mooring fee is charged. For those who want to spend time on the beach, the staithe at Horsey Mere is just over a mile away from the beach.

Back To The Bure

Having sailed back down the Thurne, why not rejoin the Bure, heading upstream towards Horning and Wroxham. The remains of St Benet's Abbey has become one of the best known Broadland landmarks and lies a few bends up river from Thurne Mouth. For those who want a closer look, there are good public moorings up-

river of the Abbey. It was founded, by King Canute, as a Benedictine Order, in 1020, on the site of the original monastery, which was destroyed by the Vikings in 870. The Abbey was progressively dismantled following the dissolution of the Monasteries during the Reign of Henry VIII, with the Abbey's stones being used in the construction of many local buildings. Almost opposite St Benet's Abbey lies the entrance to Fleet Dyke and South Walsham's inner and outer Broads. Although you can sail on the inner Broad it is private, with mooring, landing and fishing being forbidden.

The River Ant

Returning briefly to the Bure, the next point of interest is the entrance to the River Ant. The first landmark is the fixed bridge at Ludham (8.5ft air draft). There are good moorings either side of the bridge to raise/lower your mast, as well as a small shop. It is quite a long walk to Ludham itself, so those interested in visiting the village should sail to Womack Water off the River Thurne. The River Ant, between Ludham and Barton Broad, is a pretty stretch of water running mostly through open marshland with reed-lined river banks.

Barton Broad could be described as the jewel in the crown of the Northern "zone", following its extensive restoration by the Broads Authority. By the early 1990s, the Broad had silted up, while the water quality had deteriorated considerably. In 1996, the Broads Authority embarked on a 5 year programme of suction dredging. As well as improving the water quality, the most obvious benefit of this work to the yachtsman is the greater depth of water, both inside and outside the marked channel. At the top of Barton Broad you can either follow the Ant up to the fixed bridge at Wayford (7ft air draft), or sail on to Sutton Broad and the 24 hour free moorings at Sutton Staithe. Alternatively, you could head north from Sutton Broad and sail up Stalham Dyke into the village of Stalham which is home to various boatyards and the Museum of the Broads.

Back To The Bure Again

For those returning to the Bure from the Ant, the next point of interest is the entrance to Ranworth and Malthouse Broads, known as Ranworth Dam. The name is appropriate because it leads boats into Malthouse Broad and straight past the sealed off Ranworth Broad. Public moorings are available at the staithe that has a number of public facilities, including a Broads Authority information centre, a children's playground, a public telephone, and toilets, as well as the Malsters pub. For the more adventurous, Ranworth Church's tower provides one of the best views of the Broads. As you rejoin the Bure from Ranworth, the trees become more numerous as you approach the picturesque village of Horning with its large number of thatched cottages and boathouses. There

One of the pretty thatched buildings that line the banks of the River Bure as it flows through Horning. © Richard Johnstone-Bryden

are a number of good moorings, including those by Horning Ferry Inn, Horning Ferry Marina and the parish staithe. Perhaps the most unusual boat to be found cruising from Horning is the Mississippi style paddle steamer *Southern Comfort* that is used throughout the summer to give short river trips to countless holiday makers. The village's facilities include shops, public telephones and toilets, as well as a slipway capable of taking anything up to and including a Norfolk Wherry.

As you clear Horning you quickly come across the entrance to Black Horse Broad. This tranquil piece of water came to symbolise the dispute between local landowners and the public over rights of access to private Broads. During the 19th Century a number of Norfolk Landowners sealed off their Broads from the main river network under the auspices of the Enclosures Acts and Awards. Since time immemorial all Broadland waters had been considered as part of the King's River and thus were free and common to all men. Disgusted by the direct challenge to these ancient rights Norfolk boatbuilder and designer Herbert Woods led the public campaign to confront this behaviour, resulting in the "invasion" of Black Horse Broad in March

Dydlers Mill is now a highly desirable riverside home.

© Richard Johnstone-Bryden

1949. Herbert Woods, together with 30 local men, used a former landing craft to dismantle the barrier of tree trunks and chains at the entrance to the Broad. As a result of this act of direct action, an agreement was reached whereby the owner of the Broad agreed to open the water to the public each year between Easter and mid September. Sadly, this campaign did not lead to the re-opening of other closed Broads, such as Hoveton Great Broad.

The Bure between Horning and Wroxham becomes increasingly sheltered by the trees either side of the river, thus making it somewhat frustrating at times to sail up these beauti-ful stretches. There are two Broads between Black Horse Broad and Wroxham that are open to the public. The first of these is Salhouse Broad with its grassy slopes and sandy hills, making a change from the usual Broadland scenery. The second is the much larger Wroxham Broad - home of the Norfolk Broads Yacht Club. Although visiting boats can sail on the Broad, you should keep clear of the racing course at weekends when it is in use by the members. For those wanting to watch the racing, you should use a mud weight to moor along the edge of the Broad out of the way. Do not use any of the mooring buoys, because

Broads yachts racing on Wroxham Broad. © Richard Johnstone-Bryden

these are private.

The tree-lined river from Wroxham Broad soon gives way to a series of waterside properties as you sail into the village of Wroxham itself. Moorings are difficult to find within Wroxham, although there are 24 hour moorings on the western side of Wroxham Road Bridge (air draft 7.75ft), close to the Broads Authority Information Centre. Temporary moorings are available close to the eastern side of the bridge, for those needing to drop their masts to pass under the bridge. Wroxham is home to a number of boatyards, many of which operate hire fleets of motor cruisers. There are also a variety of shops, including Roys of Wroxham which was once described as the world's largest village shop. Having passed under the Wroxham Railway bridge (air draft 15ft), you can sail up the remaining navigable part of the Bure to Coltishall, with difficulty. The attractive village has good public moorings along the common, its facilities comprising pubs, shops (including a few antique shops), a garage and post office. The end of navigation is slightly upstream of the common at Coltishall Lock.

The trading wherry *Albion* uses Oulton Broad's Mutford Lock, which is one of two points of entry to the Broads from the North Sea.

© Richard Johnstone-Bryden

The Southern Rivers

The Southern "zone" of the Broads is made up of the Rivers Yare, Wensum, Chet and Waveney. These rivers were once the commercial hub of the Broads with the movement of cargoes from both Great Yarmouth and Lowestoft to Norwich. Originally, these cargoes were moved by Norfolk Keels, that gave way to Norfolk Wherries, which in turn gave way to road and rail transport. In addition to the sailing craft, small coasters were used in the 20th century, including most recently the 62 metre tanker *Blackheath*. Despite the demise of these commercial activities, the ports of Great Yarmouth and Lowestoft still provide the two points of entry to the Broads from the North Sea.

Nigel Royall's model of a Norfolk Keel. The Keel preceded the Norfolk Wherry as a cargo vessel plying the Broads.

© Richard Johnstone-Bryden

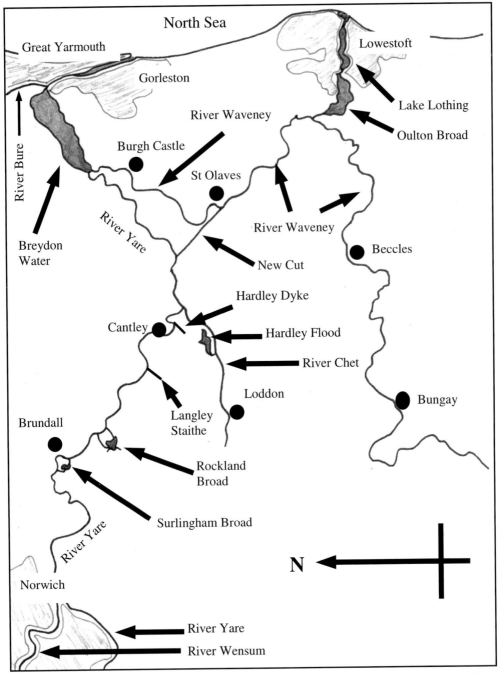

Above: Sketch showing main features of the Southern Rivers. The River Yare once carried coastal cargo vessels as far inland as Norwich. Wherries once navigated the River Waveney inland as far as Bungay.

© Seaquest Associates

30

The Broads yacht *Henriette* passes *Dragonfly* on the lower stretches of the River Yare.
© Richard Johnstone-Bryden

The River Yare

The River Yare's first landmark, for those joining from Breydon Water, is the remote Berney Arms pub which provides a good staging point for boats, either heading to, or returning from, Great Yarmouth. The river between Berney Arms and Reedham runs through open marshland and there are no moorings along the mainly reed-lined banks. Before you reach Reedham itself you will have to pass through the Reedham Swing Bridge. Normally, this bridge will open fairly quickly, providing the bridgeman is not waiting for a train. If the bridge is going to be closed for some time the river can become quite congested with boats jostling for position in the relatively strong tidal waters close to the bridge. Therefore, it is always better to pick a holding position slightly further down the river, away from the other boats. During hot weather it is best to clear Reedham either at the beginning, or the end, of the day because the expansion of the metal structure sometimes prevents the bridge being opened in the afternoon. There are plenty of moorings along Reedham's quay and the village has a Post Office, local shops and the Lord Nelson pub. If you are looking for a good place to eat, the nearby pub at Reedham Ferry is worth a visit with its

Above: The pleasure wherry *Hathor* passes through the railway swing bridge at Reedham.

both photographs, © Richard Johnstone-Bryden

Below: Water skiers are still permitted to use some stretches of the River Yare and River Waveney. The behaviour of the skiers using this section of the River Yare between Cantley and Brundall has improved dramatically in recent years.

Above: The southern edge of Rockland Broad.

Below: Pull's Ferry, River Wensum, Norwich.

combination of good food and overnight moorings. The chain ferry at Reedham is the last of its kind on the Broads and you should aim to pass over the chains at the mid point between the ferry and the bank.

From Reedham, the next point of interest along the river is the entrance to the 3.5 mile long River Chet. This narrow twisting river is one of the most frustrating stretches of water on the Broads, seeming to go on forever. The Chet is best tackled under power as there is little room to manoeuvre if you meet a large motor cruiser coming the other way. The ordeal of navigating up the River Chet is more than compensated by the small market town of Loddon, with its collection of shops, and diminishing number of boatyards. There are free 24 hour moorings at Chedgrave and along the Town Quay where boats are required to moor stern-to.

The River Yare between Reedham and Buckenham Ferry offers the most satisfying sailing grounds for the true yachtsmen, with long wide stretches that seem to go on for ever. The only downside is the sugar beet factory at Cantley, which is an eyesore and smells most unpleasant during the sugar beet season at the end of the year. The secluded Langley Staithe offers good sheltered moorings off the main River Yare. However there are no longer facilities there, so the pubs at Cantley, or Buckenham Ferry, may prove to be a better option. Along some stretches of the river, between Cantley and Brundall, you will encounter water skiers at certain times. These water skiers were once a menace to other users but they have dramatically improved their behaviour and are considerate to other boats, giving them a wide berth as they go past. However, anglers pose a much bigger problem to yachtsmen along this part of the river, with their long rods reducing these wide stretches to a small navigable channel. Anglers also use moorings as a staging but they normally move without any problems if you want to moor up.

Above Buckenham Ferry you will discover Rockland Broad. Despite its large expanse of open water, the Broad is quite shallow and you should keep to the clearly marked channel at all times. However, if you have a small rowing boat, or a shallow draft dinghy, you can take advantage of this great stretch of water and even go hunting for wherry wrecks along the southern edge of the Broad. At the top of the Broad there is a short dyke that leads to the village pub and public staithe. This short passage should be approached with care by yachts, because the overhanging tree branches leave little room for manoeuvre when meeting boats coming the other way.

The last major centre of population before Norwich is the riverside village of Brundall. Despite the rather Heath Robinson appearance of Brundall's river front, the growing village is home to a number of boatyards, marine equipment suppliers, and a marina. Although the village has a number of shops and other useful facilities, there are no public moorings, so those wanting to stop at this point could try the Coldham Hall pub on the opposite river bank, or the nearby Surlingham Broad which is an ideal place to drop the mud weight and stop for lunch. On the outskirts of Norwich the River Yare joins the River Wensum, which flows into the heart of the city. Moorings are available at the Norwich Yacht Station, but those wanting a quiet night should avoid the weekend because the revellers leaving the various clubs in the early hours can be very noisy. This historic city is currently experiencing a period of sustained regeneration with a number of major building projects, either underway, or recently completed, so it is well worth a visit with its numerous shops and cultural attractions. The city centre is approximately 10 - 15 minutes walk from the Yacht Station.

The River Waveney

On joining the River Waveney from Breydon Water, the first visible land mark is the ruined Roman fort of Burgh Castle which is worth a visit if you can moor at the nearby public moorings. The river between Burgh Castle and the small village of St Olaves runs through open marshland. Like the lower stretches of the River Yare the insides of bends should be approached with caution on a falling tide, because many of them are fairly shallow as a result of silting. There are boatyards along the river bank either side of the fixed metal road bridge but those needing to drop their mast should use the public moorings on the northern bank. A stop here has the added benefit of providing an opportunity to buy provi-

The remains of the Roman Foreshore Fort, Burgh Castle.

© Richard Johnstone-Bryden

sions at one of the two local shops. There are also moorings on the other side of the bridge at the Bell Inn, but boats are required to moor stern-to.

Having cleared St Olaves you could either continue to head south, or you could sail down the New Cut, to join up with the River Yare at Reedham. The New Cut was created in the early 19th Century to provide a direct water-borne link between Lowestoft and Norwich for the movement of cargoes. Today the cut is becoming increasingly shallow, and those sailing from the east, who need to drop their masts while alongside should do so at Somerleyton because the depth

of water at the moorings by Haddiscoe bridge is now only about 3ft.

The River Waveney between St Olaves and Oulton Dyke runs through more open marshland with reed-lined banks. About the only interruption to this remote landscape is the small village of Somerleyton, indicated principally by the swing railway bridge and the small marina on the St Olaves side of the bridge. The bridgemen usually open this bridge fairly quickly unless they are waiting for a train. If the bridge is closed, it is always best to pick a holding position away from the bridge and only begin your approach when the bridge

Oulton Week is one of the two biggest regattas held on the Broads.

The wherry yacht *White Moth* heads up the River Waveney towards Beccles.

is open, as this leaves room for those boats that can pass underneath the bridge. Water Skiers also use parts of the river between Somerleyton and Oulton Dyke at certain times.

If you like remote riverside moorings there are a few along Oulton Dyke, before it opens out into the main Broad itself. Oulton Broad is unique within the Broadland network because it enables members of the public to witness the spectacle of yacht racing or powerboat racing from Nicholas Everitt Park, which runs along the southern bank of the Broad. The Broad itself is the main attraction for visitors, and the best way to enjoy being on the Broad is to rent a mooring buoy from the Harbour Master. Alternatively, you could moor up at the Yacht Station, which has a choice of alongside, or stern-to moorings. For those with limited washing facilities on their boat, the Yacht Station has baths and showers, as well as washing machines and tumble driers. The village's facilities include a small supermarket, two train stations, a nearby petrol station and a good public slip capable of taking most trailer launched boats. Chandlery is available from the well stocked shop Jeckells, which also offers rigging, upholstery and cover making services.

The river between Oulton Dyke and the market town of Beccles is, in my opinion, the most beautiful part of the Waveney. The closer you get to Beccles the reed-lined banks give way to grassy meadows and more densely wooded areas. You can moor up on the Oulton side of the fixed road bridge at Beccles, but it is about 10 to 15 minutes walk into the town. The absence of any lighting at night means that I would recommend dropping the mast and mooring up at the Yacht Station. This attractive town is certainly worth a visit with its good selection of shops and pubs. The more adventurous can continue their voyage beyond Beccles to Geldeston Lock, which marks the limit of navigation on the River Waveney.

Local Events

The Broads is home to over 900 indigenous traditional sailing craft. One of the best opportunities to see these boats in action is at the various events held around the Broads during the summer months.

Power boat racing on Oulton Broad.   © Richard Johnstone-Bryden

On the Southern Rivers

Four different annual events provide an insight into the different types of racing held on the southern rivers. The biggest of these occasions is Oulton Week, now held in mid August and hosted by the Waveney & Oulton Broad Yacht Club. The regatta has a packed programme of racing that caters for all of the types of classic Broadland sailing craft. Breydon Regatta is organised by the Yare Sailing Club, and held in August, on Breydon Water. Racing is only open to the River Cruiser Class and, because of its location, the only way to see the racing is by boat. Beccles Regatta is also held in August, hosted by the Beccles Amateur Sailing Club. There is daily racing for both the Waveney ODs and the Norfolk Dinghy ODs in the somewhat narrow waters of the River Waveney, which provides some interesting moments for competitor and spectator alike. The Yare Navigation Race is organised by Coldham Sailing Club and is open to all traditional Broads yachts. The 30 mile passage race starts at Coldham Hall and competing yachts make their way down to the half way mark on Breydon Water. Spectators can see the progress of this exciting race at various points along the Yare, including Buckenham Ferry and Reedham Ferry.

Heigham Sound during the annual 3 Rivers Race.

© Richard Johnstone-Bryden

powerboat racing is organised throughout the summer months by the Lowestoft & Oulton Broad Motor Boat Club. The sight of racing boats reaching speeds of up 100 mph on Oulton Broad can be seen most Thursday evenings, with larger race meetings held on a few weekends. To ensure the highest levels of safety for competitors and river users alike, most of the Broad becomes prohibited territory for the duration of these races, although a channel is kept clear along the northern bank to allow boats to enter or leave Oulton Broad.

On the Northern Rivers

Not surprisingly, there is also a full diary of fixtures held around the Northern "zone" during the summer months. Four events best illustrate the breadth of racing to be found on these waters. Wroxham Week is one of the two biggest events on the Broads and is hosted by the Norfolk Broads Yacht Club. It has racing for most types of traditional Broadland sailing craft, with an average annual turn out of at least 100 classic boats. The 3 Rivers Race starts from Horning and is one of the major spectator events, with people often hanging around either Acle or Potter Heigham bridge well into the evening to watch each of the competing craft "shoot the

40

Yare & Bure One Designs competing in the annual Horning Week Regatta.   © Richard Johnstone-Bryden

bridge". The event attracts many different types of competitor, including classic Broads yachts and the various One Designs. Thurne Mouth Open Regatta is perhaps one of the most challenging events because it is held at the main junction for craft moving about the Broads. This can lead to some heart stopping moments for competitors jostling for position among various hire craft. Finally, Horning Sailing Club hosts a week-long regatta at the beginning of August. Like the Beccles Regatta, Horning Week is a very relaxed family event, with racing for Broads yachts, Yare & Bure One Designs, Rebel One Designs and Reedlings, as well as modern keel boats and dinghies.

Even in the hottest weather Percy Hunter was always smartly turned
out for work - never appearing without a collar and tie.

via Jennifer Mack

The three founders of Hunter's Fleet (left to right) Stanley, Cyril and Percy Hunter.

via Jennifer Mack

Chapter Two

A Leap Of Faith

Percy Hunter & Sons 1932 - 1968

Behind the tranquil facade of Hunter's Yard lies a story of enormous risk, determination and sheer hard work that began amid some of the worst economic conditions to be faced by Great Britain during the 20th Century. For many Broadland boatbuilders the job of manager at a successful boatyard would have marked the high point of their career but for Percy Hunter, who was the Manager at George Applegate's Potter Heigham yard, it was merely a stepping stone to establishing his own boatyard to hire out high quality sailing craft. By 1931 Percy's sons Cyril and Stanley had gained enough experience of boatbuilding to be able to play a useful role within his new venture so Percy began the search for a suitable site along the banks of the northern rivers of the Norfolk Broads.

Although Percy had managed to build up some savings of his own and raise additional funds through loans, including

Stanley Hunter onboard a motor launch while he was still working for George Applegate's Potter Heigham boatyard. via Liz Witton

one from his mother-in-law, he had to be very careful how he spent every penny. It was a lesson that was to remain with Percy for the rest of his life because he always used his available funds extremely wisely to ensure that, when he had to spend money, he obtained full value. In keeping with these principles Percy decided that the most economic method of acquiring a boatyard would be to buy some land by a river and build everything from scratch, which had the added benefit of requiring less money up front. Following their unsuccessful

attempt to acquire some land on the edge of Black Horse Broad, Percy entered into negotiations with the farmer Charles Green to purchase some open marshland at the end of Ludham's Horsefen Road. In those days Horsefen Road was mainly used during the sugar beet season, when the crop was delivered to Womack Staithe to be loaded onto a waiting wherry for the voyage round to the sugar beet factory at Cantley. The route was so little used during the rest of the year that grass would grow up in the middle of the road! When Percy had reached an agreement to pay £200 for the land, he set up the partnership Percy Hunter & Sons, with Cyril and Stanley, prior to concluding the purchase of the land on 6 February 1932.

Once the paperwork was in place the Hunters took possession of their land, which overlooked Womack Water, and embarked on the task of transforming it into a boatyard. However, their finances did not allow all three Hunters to leave their jobs at Applegate's immediately to work full time at Ludham. As the best paid of the trio it was important for Percy to remain at Potter Heigham for as long as possible to provide

Pat Thrower and Cyril Hunter (right) widen the dyke. Like the initial excavation work to create the main dyke this later digging was carried out entirely by hand. *via Jennifer Mack*

the much needed cash flow to pay the expenses until the arrival of the first paying customers. Unfortunately, there are no records of when the Hunters left Applegate's, but it is known that Cyril was the first of the trio to leave Potter Heigham. Unlike Stanley, Cyril had already completed his boatbuilding apprenticeship enabling him to work without Percy's constant supervision. The Hunters worked some extremely long hours during these first few months because, when they had finished their time at Potter Heigham, both Percy and Stanley provided Cyril with some much needed assistance in the evenings and at weekends.

For their first year of business the Hunters set themselves some ambitious targets. In addition to developing their Ludham site they also committed themselves to building the first three yachts, which were listed within the 1932 Blakes brochure. However, before the keel of the first yacht could be laid, the Hunters had to undertake the gruelling task of excavating a dyke by hand to link Womack Water with the site of the future boatsheds. This work was prompted by their discov-

The four berth yacht *Lustre* was the first yacht to be built by the Hunters at Ludham.

via Jennifer Mack

ery that the land along the edge of Womack Water was not capable of supporting a building without very deep foundations. When they carefully surveyed the rest of the land with sounding rods they came across an extremely firm clay pad about 250ft away from the water which was about four feet below the surface. This pad was almost as hard as concrete and quite capable of supporting a structure up to the size of the two sheds that now form Hunter's Yard. In effect the area surrounding this pad was like a gigantic saucer with the clay collecting at the bottom. Even though the additional expense of creating this dyke was unwelcome news, it did have

the benefit of providing a set of moorings that were protected from the traffic using Womack Water.

Prior to the start of digging, a 30ft long dam had to be built in front of the stretch of bank where the dyke would join Womack Water to prevent the water breaking through and flooding the new channel ahead of its completion. The two inch wide wooden boards were grooved along one edge and sharpened on the other so that they would fit tightly together. The bottom of each board was pointed so that they could be easily driven into the river bed to complete the seal. To keep the planks firmly together the dam was finished off with a

40ft long baulk of timber which was secured along the length of the dam in the middle. Once the dam was completed the digging work had to be carried out as quickly as possible in case the water broke through to flood the channel before it was finished. Therefore, both Percy and Stanley took three weeks leave from Applegate's to carry out the work together with Cyril, Percy's older brother Harry, the local undertaker Pat Thrower, known as "Dumbo", and another labourer. In addition to the excavation work the men also built a slipway using railway sleepers at the end of the dyke where the boatsheds would subsequently be built. As the team's work edged ever closer to the dam the small amount of water seeping through the bank into the channel was kept in check by an outboard motor geared up to a turbine pump. By the time the men finished their arduous task they had created a channel measuring 250ft by 30ft with a depth of 4ft along its entire length.

The sequence of events following the completion of the dyke are somewhat unclear because the surviving documentary evidence clearly challenges the previously accepted version of the founding of Hunter's Yard and its hire fleet. For example, it was firmly believed that Percy bought the land for the Yard in 1931, whereas the Deeds for the Yard clearly show that the land was not purchased from Charles Green of Beech Farm, Ludham until 6 February 1932. This point is backed up in an oath given by Cyril Hunter in December 1967. In this document he clearly states that Percy did not take possession of the land until soon after its purchase in 1932. Cyril also states that the dyke was excavated shortly after the Hunters took possession of the land thereby giving us a date of February, or March, for the creation of the dyke. It was also thought that when the dyke was completed the Hunters started work on the first shed. However, Smallburgh Rural District Council did not formally grant planning permission for the first shed until August 1933. This of course raises the immediate question of where *Lustre* and *Lullaby* were built. There is no evidence to contradict the firmly held view that they were built at Ludham, so the most likely option is that the Hunters erected some form of temporary structure, which was either enlarged or replaced.

Each of the Hunter yachts have a relatively simple uncluttered interior. In keeping with the majority of Broads yachts additional headroom is provided by the lifting roof.

Photographs © Richard Johnstone-Bryden

Originally each of the Hunter yachts were fitted with two primus stoves in the cooker locker located under a cockpit seat. These stoves were subsequently replaced by gas cookers like this one.

The origins of each design have also led to a certain amount of speculation, not least whether or not any of the boats were based on an existing yacht. Without the ability to consult the Hunter trio themselves it is fair to say that all three of them would have been involved in the creation of each class. By virtue of his greater experience of boatbuilding Percy would have led the design process, with Cyril and Stanley making their contributions as appropriate. In general terms the Hunter designs follow the basic characteristics of the Broads yachts built during the inter-war years, in that they have a spoon bow, transom stern, carvel planking, lifting cabin roof and a counter-balanced mast mounted in a tabernacle. Inside they are lit by gimballed oil lamps and the cooking was originally done on two primus stoves located in a locker in the cockpit well. Although the first bermudan rigged yachts were beginning to appear on the Broads, Percy equipped each of his yachts with a gaff rig because it provides the best all round performance in the conditions encountered around the Broads. However, he decided to use a small self tacking jib rather

Soon after *Lustre* was completed it was decided that she should be hired out with a dinghy so within a fortnight Percy Hunter had completed a tender for her.

via Jim Searle

than a larger loose footed jib because he saw bowsprits as an unnecessary source of damage both to the boat itself as well as other people's boats. In keeping with the style of the yachts that Percy built when he was at Applegate's, such as the two Brownies, he opted for mahogany planking on oak frames. Obviously, there was nothing to stop Percy painting the hulls but, in reality, those yards that chose mahogany planking usually varnished the hulls to show off the quality and beauty of the wood. Little did Percy realise

Each of the 4 berth yachts were allocated an 11ft sailing / rowing dinghy. Initially the dinghy was supplied as part of the standard package before Blakes suggested that the dinghy should be hired as an additional service.

© Peter Hollingham / NCC

that the high grade finish of his yacht's varnish was to become a trademark of the Yard, especially as the number of boats with varnished hulls progressively diminished in Broadland waters during the post war years.

To help maximise the income from their early customers, the Hunters concentrated on building their biggest yachts first. In reality there would have been little genuine difference between the construction costs of the four and three berth yachts, but the revenue generated by the additional berth onboard the larger yachts was very important. Sadly, there is no record of when work began on *Lustre* and *Lullaby* but it is firmly believed that *Lustre* was the first of the pair to be built. The 1933 Blakes brochure confirms that *Lustre* and *Lullaby* were completed in 1932, and this fact is backed up by a photograph of either *Lustre* or *Lullaby* as part of their entry within that brochure. Shortly after *Lustre* was completed it was decided that she should be hired out with a dinghy as the tender so, within a fortnight, Percy had finished a dinghy for her. In the early years each yacht was hired out with its own tender but Blakes later suggested that this should become an additional charged service. Each 4 berth yacht was allocated with one 11ft rowing / sailing dinghy, while 9 ft rowing dinghies were assigned to the other yachts.

Despite their apparent appetite for hard work, there was a limit to how much the Hunters could realistically achieve within their first season, so Percy placed a contract with

Woodruff was unique within the Hunter's Fleet in that she was the only yacht to be fitted with portholes.　　　via Mr G.L. Oakenfold

Alfred Pegg of Wroxham to build the third yacht. Pegg's Yard was short of work at the time so Percy was able to negotiate a good price for the yacht's construction. As completed, *Woodruff* was the first of the three berth Wood Class yachts and closely resembled the two Brownies built by Applegate's when Percy was the Manager. Closer inspection of both designs reveal that they have very similar dimensions. However, the layout of the forward half of *Woodruff's* interior differed considerably from the scheme adopted for the two Brownies. In the earlier pair of yachts the forward berth is fitted across the width of the boat, with the heads and wash basin located between the forward berth and the two aft berths. The arrangements for the forward half of the Wood Class accommodation made better use of the available space by having the third berth running fore and aft while the heads and wash basin were located on the opposite side. *Woodruff* was unique within the class in having her berth on the portside and the heads etc on the starboard side. The most obvious explanation for this is that the tracing of the plans supplied to Alfred Pegg was reproduced the wrong way round. This view is reinforced by the fact that the interior plan, used within the 1932 Blakes catalogue, shows the forward berth on the starboard side like the later Ludham-built yachts. It is also quite likely that *Woodruff* was in fact a transitional yacht, between the design for the Brownies and the subsequent Ludham-built boats, thus explaining a number of the other minor differences. For example, *Woodruff* was fitted with portholes in her cabin sides, like the Brownies, whereas the later Wood Class yachts all had oval windows, with sliding glass running within externally mounted wooden rails. Presumably, this subsequent arrangement was used because it was significantly cheaper and much easier to replace in the event of an accident. However, there was one difference that was a direct result of where she was constructed. Like all Pegg's creations, *Woodruff* has a much flatter sheerline than the yachts built by the Hunters.

Like *Lustre* and *Lullaby*, *Woodruff's* completion date is confirmed by the 1933 Blakes brochure, which also includes a good sailing shot of her as part of her description within the brochure. Even though the Hunters needed to attract as many hirers as possible they exhibited an interesting attitude towards their clients. Instead of being grateful for their custom, the Hunters ensured that their clients felt it was an honour and a privilege to be allowed to charter their boats! This message was reinforced by the entry for the 4 berth yachts within the Blakes brochure, which ends with the sentences "The finish compares with that found in the best private craft. They are intended for those clients who really take a pride in their craft." Some hirers responded to this attitude by spending the final night of their holiday frantically cleaning their boat before they returned it to the Yard on Saturday morning to ensure that they were allowed to come back the following year! Not surprisingly, there was a list of people who were banned from hiring yachts again. This punishment was usually reserved for those crews who seriously damaged a boat, left the interior covered in mud, or walked on the sails when they were being lowered. Friday night was always an anxious time for the Hunters, because they never knew in what state the boats would be returned, but these feelings soon turned to relief when they discovered that there were no major repairs to complete.

Above: The calm before the storm! A full dyke at Hunter's Yard as the yachts await their next set of hirers on a Saturday morning.

Both photographs via Jennifer Mack

Below: The few hours between the departing and incoming hirers on a Saturday morning always provided the Hunters with a brief opportunity to carry out minor work on the yachts to keep them up to scratch. Here Cyril is quickly working on *Lustre* in the Yard before she goes out on hire again.

Cyril talks to one of the customers as they join a *Hustler* at the start of their holiday. *via Jennifer Mack*

Changeover day itself was always a hectic time at the Yard. Percy would spend much of the time talking to the hirers, many of whom became firm friends of the family over the years. Cyril and Stanley would check each yacht as it was returned and complete any necessary repairs before the linen and crockery were changed for the next set of hirers. Before WWII Percy's wife Ethel would look after the domestic side of the yachts. As part of her weekly routine on a Saturday morning she would polish the glasses, shake and fold the blankets, as well as changing the sheets, pillow cases, tea towels, and generally dust the cabins. As the number of yachts increased, Ethel was helped out each week by Stanley's wife Phyllis following their marriage in September 1937. Providing the yachts had been returned undamaged and on time they were normally ready for collection by the next set of hirers early in the afternoon. In the 1930s many customers travelled to Wroxham by train, before hiring a taxi for the short journey to Ludham. The arrival of any hirers who said they had not sailed before always caused an enormous sense of alarm. In later years the Hunters would usually go up to the loft by the

Wood Sorrel on Wroxham Broad 10th September 1933.

via Jim Searle

office to observe the performance of such clients through
Stanley's powerful pair of bin-
oculars, which originally came
from the conning tower of a
Japanese submarine, as they
headed off down the River
Thurne. Among the "crimes"
guaranteed to annoy Percy were
people sailing with all the fenders down and those who did not
pull up the mainsail high
enough.

The Hunters kept up their
busy schedule as they entered
their second year of business.
The building programme for
that year included the third 4
berth yacht *Luna*, the second 3
berth yacht *Wood Sorrel*, and
the Fleet's first half decker

Woodcut. Percy built *Woodcut*
himself and she closely resembled the half deckers *Sunrise*
and *Sunset* which had been
built by Applegates during his
time there. She was to become
his favourite boat within the
Fleet and he would often take
her out on his own for the day.
Depending on the prevailing
conditions he would usually
take a picnic together with his
fishing rod and head off towards South Walsham. Once
the boatbuilding programme for
1933 had been completed the
Hunters turned their attention to
building their first permanent
boat shed before the growing
fleet had to be slipped for their
winter maintenance. Although

55

Above: The first boat shed under construction.   via Jim Searle

Below: The first boatshed shortly after it was completed.
via Tom Grapes

Above: Looking out across Hunter's Yard from the site of the second boatshed.

Below: Hunter's Yard after the completion of the second boatshed with *Luna* in the foreground.

Most of the Hunter yachts were built in the "building berth" at the top of the original boatshed. The same position has since been used for the restorations of *Brown Bess* and *Rebel Reveller* as well as the construction of new 4 berth yacht.   via Jim Searle

the Hunter's hire season, of Easter through to late September, may seem short by modern hire fleet standards it provided the Hunters with enough time to overhaul the yachts properly. The early slipping of the yachts also ensured that they were not exposed to the risk of frost damage, which could significantly increase the maintenance programme in return for limited bookings. It is thanks in part to these well thought out routines, maintained to the present day, that the Fleet has managed to survive so well for over seven decades.

Because of the time devoted to building the first shed in 1933, followed by the second shed in 1935, the Hunters only managed to build *Wood Violet* and *Wood Rose* in 1934 and 1935 respectively. However, they were able to manage a higher rate of production when they launched the first two Hustlers in 1936. These two berth yachts are the most elegant of the Hunter designs as the space, freed up by the deletion of the third berth of the Wood Class, enabled Percy to create a more balanced set of lines. Like the other two classes of yacht

Percy Hunter was less than impressed when he saw this stunning photograph of a Hustler. He was extremely displeased at the way one of his yachts was being treated!

via Jim Searle

within the Fleet the Hustlers handle very well and are more like overgrown dinghies to sail. Indeed when Percy was once asked to explain why his yachts sailed so well he simply replied, "they were designed to sail on the water and not through it."

Sadly, there are no records to establish when the remaining Hustlers were completed because Blakes do not refer to the number of Hustlers available for hire until their 1938 brochure, in which Hustlers 1 - 4 are listed. Although Blakes do not include *Hustler 5*

within their 1939 brochure, the small catalogue printed on behalf of the Yard for the 1939 season does include *Hustler 5* therefore giving us a probable completion date for *Hustler 5* of 1939.

In addition to the Hustlers, Cyril built the second Woodcut Class half decker in 1938. The Hunters purchased their wood from Taylor's of Wroxham. Percy would pick out a log and have it sawn into planks before it was delivered to Ludham, where it was laid plank upon plank to resemble a log again. To allow even drying

Woodcut 2 under construction.

the planks were separated by splines at 6ft intervals. The wood was covered with a tarpaulin and left outside the shed to season. To ensure he managed to purchase the best wood Percy would often call into Taylor's Yard to see what timber they had in stock. During one of these routine visits some very high quality mahogany, that had been earmarked for use within railway carriages, immediately caught Percy's eye. He was determined to acquire this wood for his next half decker so he tried to persuade Reggie Taylor to sell him the log. Eventually, Taylor gave into Percy's persistent requests and agreed to sell him enough timber from this log to build *Woodcut 2*. When Cyril made the planks for the hull the wood was of such high quality that he was able to make the planks fit close enough to eliminate the need for caulking.

Just when the Hunters seemed to have got their business onto a level keel, international events looked as though they were about to disturb the way of life in Ludham. As the hire season reached it peak in August 1939 the prospect of a major European war became increasingly likely. Unlike the First World War, it looked as though the imminent conflict

To disguise the location of Hunter's Yard from German bombers the boatshed roofs were painted with camouflage. Basil King is in the foreground and Cyril is kneeling while Stanley is wearing a large sun hat. The other two workers are unknown.   via Jennifer Mack

would have a very real impact upon the Broadland hire industry. Rumours began to circulate that, in the event of war, all available boats would be seized as part of the anti invasion measures, and anchored on open stretches of water to prevent enemy seaplanes from landing. Percy was determined to avoid the confiscation of his fleet by the Government so he took the bold decision to suspend his business in the middle of August and begin slipping the yachts before they could be seized. As soon as the Fleet was safely inside the sheds, the Hunters turned their attention to concealing the location of the Yard from enemy bombers by painting camouflage on the corrugated asbestos roof. These actions were to prove extremely wise because, soon after Great Britain declared war on Nazi Germany on 3 September 1939, the Government began requisitioning hire boats from boatyards around the Broads. When the Government officials finally came across Hunter's Fleet they agreed to leave the boats where they were providing a boat was sunk across the entrance to the dyke to prevent the boats from being used by German soldiers in the event of an invasion. Percy's quick thinking certainly saved the Fleet and provided him with a head start over his competitors when peace returned because many of the boats that were left out on the Broads either sank, or were in need of extensive refits before they could return to service.

In the meantime while the Fleet sat out the war in Ludham the nation desperately needed skilled boatbuilders to help the war effort. Initially, the Admiralty placed contracts with its normal suppliers to meet its increased demand for small craft, such as Motor Torpedo Boats (MTBs). The closure of Hunter's Yard meant that Cyril and Stanley had to find alternative employment so they headed south to the Thames to work for Thornycroft during the early months of the war. There was little time for relaxation as they were required to work six days a week, between 0700 and 1900. Percy stayed behind in Norfolk and went to work for Herbert Woods at Potter Heigham. When the number of contracts began to increase

from the Admiralty, Percy arranged for his sons to return to Norfolk. Fortunately, they came back a few weeks before London was bombed for the first time on 24 August 1940. The three Hunters spent the rest of the war at Potter Heigham, working on a variety of small craft, including several 72ft Harbour Defence Motor Launches (HDMLs) for the Royal Navy.

In addition to his long shifts at Potter Heigham Stanley, agreed to take on the role of Sub Officer when the Government decided to establish a part time fire station at Ludham. The volunteer fire crew consisted mainly of farm workers. Every night at least two firemen were required to sleep at the station, ready to respond to an emergency at a moment's notice. The firemen were kept fairly busy dealing with crashed aircraft, stack fires and chimney fires.

By 1944 the threat of a German invasion had passed so the Government agreed to Percy Hunter's request to reopen the Yard, but their war-related work for Herbert Woods had to take priority. Because Percy, Cyril and Stanley each had a bungalow built for them across the road from the Yard

During their time at the Potter Heigham boat yard of Herbert Woods all three Hunters worked on a number of 72ft Harbour Defence Motor Launches, including ML1058 which was completed on 8 September 1941. She is seen here in Great Yarmouth prior to her handover to the Royal Navy.   via Liz Witton

in the 1930s they were able to spend a few hours every evening working on the boats after their shifts at Potter Heigham. The blackout regulations were still in force, so blinds had to be fitted to each of the Yard's windows to comply with the requirements. These rules also applied to the yachts, so the white canvas used to fill the gap between the cabin sides and the raised cabin roof was exchanged for dark green canvas. Those wartime hirers would have experienced a very similar type of sailing holiday to the ones enjoyed by the first Victo-

rian holiday-makers in the late 19th Century. Many of the facilities along the rivers were closed, while there was a complete absence of motor cruisers as a direct result of petrol rationing.

The end of hostilities in 1945 signalled the start of a rapid decline in the size of the nation's armed forces. As part of these cuts the nearby Army barracks were closed and subsequently demolished. Once the buildings had been pulled down Percy bought some of the brick rubble to use as the surface for the floor of the second shed. He

Above: When Tom Grapes joined Hunter's Yard he also became a member of the Ludham Fire Brigade. Stanley Hunter was the Sub Officer for the fire station. The firemen were called out to pump out the trading wherry *Gleanor* at Womack Staithe in the early 1950s after she sank with a full load of sugar beet. The group by the tabernacle are (left to right) Divisional Officer Todd, two men associated with *Gleanor*, Stanley Hunter and Tom Grapes. The other man amidships is unknown but it is believed to be part of the wherry's crew.   Both photographs via Tom Grapes

Below: Cyril Hunter, Stanley Hunter and Tom Grapes at the Yard late 1940s.

Above: *Luna's* stern clearly shows the burgee flown by each of the yachts when they were owned by Norfolk County Council. This burgee was adopted in the early 1970s and used until the Fleet was purchased by Norfolk Heritage Fleet Trust in 1996.

All colour photographs © Richard Johnstone-Bryden

Below: Hunter's Yard shortly before Norfolk County Council announced its decision to sell the Fleet in 1995.

PLATE I

Above: *Hustler* on the River Thurne September 1995

PLATE II

Right: *Hustler* on the River
Thurne September 1995

Above: Generations, Ian Grapes is crewed by his son Matthew onboard
Woodcut 2 in September 1995

PLATE III

Above: Ian Grapes at the helm of *Woodcut 2*
on the River Thurne September 1995

PLATE IV

Top: The cabin of every Hunter yacht is still illuminated by a gimballed oil lamp. When Jim Searle asked hirers in the 1970s if they wanted electric lighting onboard the yachts the answer was a resounding NO!

Right: Most of the Hunter yachts proudly carry their original builder's plate.

Above: The wash basin and heads are located on the port side of the forward cabin in all of the Wood class yachts except *Woodruff*

PLATE V

Above: The third berth is located on the starboardside of the forward cabin in all of the Wood class yachts except *Woodruff*

Below: The main cabin of a *Hustler* class yacht

PLATE VI

Above: (left to right) *Hustler*, *Sundew* and *Brown Bess* on the River Bure near Oby.

Below:*Hustler* on the River Bure near Oby Dyke

PLATE VII

Above: In home waters

Plate VIII

Percy Hunter in the office which was lined with Essex board. Each morning Percy would start the day by going through the post in the office while smoking his pipe. By the time he had finished it was usually impossible to see across the office! Over the years this resulted in the Essex board gradually changing from its original pale straw colour to a similar shade of brown to teak as it absorbed the tobacco smoke. *via Jim Searle*

also bought a number of doors, which were used in the construction of the loft close to the office. To stop unwanted visitors from mooring overnight in the Yard, a boom was placed over the entrance, together with a sign stating "No Water No Petrol No Mooring" Anyone unwise enough to ignore this warning before the boom was lowered was told in no uncertain terms to seek an alternative mooring! The Yard itself was always kept to a high standard not least that the grass by the quay heading was cut short.

One of the Fleet's regular customers from London once described the Yard as the nicest moorings on the Broads. He would use the Yard as his overnight base throughout his week long holiday and only go out sailing for the day. Before setting off each day he would walk down to Percy's garden and pick one of his wife's carnations. The water was also much clearer in the dyke than it is today. Cyril's daughter Jennifer and Stanley's son Michael, who grew up in the Yard after the war, remember learning to

Looking down the side of the older boatshed - a view that is still recognisable today.

via Josie Webb

swim in the dyke because it was so clean - unthinkable now!

When Blakes was resurrected after the war the yachts of Hunter's Fleet were among those listed in their first post war brochure which was published in 1946. As the Broadland tourism industry began to pick up momentum again, Percy decided to start work on the fifth Wood Class yacht at the beginning of 1947. There is an element of uncertainty about whether *Wood Avens* or *Wood Anemone* was the fifth Wood Class yacht to be built. Tom Grapes who started work at the Yard on 1 March 1947 firmly believes that *Wood Anemone* was the fifth Wood class yacht, and thus the first yacht that he participated in the building of, whereas the accounts for 1949 clearly show the expenses for building *Wood Anemone* in that year as £313 5s 1d. This later fact is reinforced by a photograph of the launching of *Wood*

Percy Hunter balances *Wood Anemone* as she is carefully manoeuvred down the greased way prior to being launched for the first time in 1949.   via Jennifer Mack

Anemone which has a hand written note by Cyril's wife Muriel on the back stating that *Wood Anemone* was launched in 1949. Unfortunately, the Blakes brochures for this period fail to provide any firm evidence because they do not list either yacht until the early 1950s. Therefore, in the absence of more conclusive evidence it looks as though *Wood Avens* was the fifth Wood Class yacht to be built.

Before Tom Grapes joined the Yard he had served in the Royal Marines and been employed as a gardener by the businessman, Mr Adcock, who was a tobacco merchant in Norwich. Mr Adcock helped to nurture Tom's lifelong interest in sailing because he would often ask Tom to crew onboard his half decker *Wind Rush* which had been built by Ernest Woods. *Wind Rush's* design closely resembled a Y&BOD except that she had a lifting keel as opposed to the fixed keel of a Y&BOD. Stanley already knew Tom so he didn't face a conventional interview, but he was given the job on the understanding that he would also join the Ludham Fire Brigade!

As Tom observed, the

Lullaby on Oulton Broad in 1947.   via Jim Searle

three Hunters had carved up the responsibility for different aspects of the business between them, according to their respective strengths. Percy provided the overall leadership and direction for the company. On a day to day basis Percy would look after the bookings and the rigging. He was always smartly dressed - never appearing for work without a collar and tie. Percy would begin each day by going through the morning post and, by the time he finished, the office was quite often full of smoke. Percy was a perfectionist and could be quite a hard task master but he was also a fair man to work for. In a crisis he seemed unflappable and,

while everyone else was rushing around, he would come out of the office, puff on his pipe, before saying few words to get things under control again. He seemed to take old age in his stride, he puffed a little more on his pipe and talked a little more, but his apparent deafness did not prevent him from hearing what he wanted to hear!

Cyril was the more outgoing of the Hunter brothers and would enjoy taking out one of the yachts on a windy day to put the fear of god into anyone unfortunate enough to be driving a motor cruiser. Cyril's time keeping was always a bit suspect and Stanley would sometimes call at Cyril's house

Wannick participating in a regatta at Potter Heigham soon after her completion.

via Jennifer Mack

in the morning to chivvy him up. At the Yard Cyril undertook the majority of the wood working duties. The two brothers undertook their fair share of call outs to sort out hirers whenever they got into difficulty. This could provide an unwelcome disruption to family life. On one such occasion Stanley had been due to take his daughter Elizabeth to the railway station to leave on a school trip to France but he received a telephone call from a hirer to say that they were stuck on Breydon Water. This resulted in Elizabeth being dropped off at the station an hour earlier than planned enabling Stanley to go off to help the hirers. In addition to helping out with all the duties around the Yard Stanley dealt with the administration in the evenings, while in the win-

ter he would do much of the varnishing, painting and sign writing.

Tom soon discovered the grim conditions endured by the staff during the winter months. The only source of heat came from the small pot belly stove located between the two sheds which failed to heat more than the immediate area around it. The rest of the Yard was so cold that ice would form in the tins of varnish! As if that was not enough, the sheds would usually flood more than once during the winter months, and all the equipment had to be kept off the floor to avoid it being damaged. As the most junior member of the staff, Tom's involvement in the construction of *Wood Avens* was limited to basic tasks such as holding on to the copper nails as they were clinched. *Wood Avens* is unique among the Hunter yachts in having a cast iron keel because lead was so expensive to buy immediately after the war. It was for this reason that some large offshore racing yachts were broken up at this time so that their owners could sell their lead keel. Not surprisingly the Hunters decided to fit a cast iron keel to *Wood Avens*. In the period between the building of *Wood Avens* and *Wood Anemone* the price of lead began to drop so the Hunters started buying odd lumps of scrap lead so that they could cast a lead keel and mast counter weight for *Wood Anemone*. The launching of *Wood Anemone* brought the Fleet up to 14 yachts and 2 half deckers. This was the maximum number of boats that could be effectively handled by the facilities at the Yard and the building of further boats for the Fleet would have required an expansion of the Yard, as well as an increase in the work force. The Hunters had worked hard to reach this point and they did not have the appetite for another phase of expansion.

However, this was not to mark the end of boatbuilding at Ludham because Cyril and Stanley decided to build themselves a boat called *Wannick*, which is Ludham slang for Womack. The brothers based their design on a Flying 15 and had high hopes for their new creation. Following her launch, the Hunter brothers hoisted her sails prior to heading out on to the River Thurne to see how she handled. Percy left the Yard sometime later in *Woodcut* and quickly overtook the new boat. Cyril and Stanley were unimpressed with the performance of *Wannick* and tried out various modifications to her rig to improve her performance before eventually laying her up in the Yard. She was subsequently sold off some years later.

As the numbers of motor cruisers within the various Broadland hire fleets began to steadily increase during the 1950s Blakes tried to persuade the Hunters to follow suit and introduce some motor cruisers to the Fleet. Although Blakes could see the overall trend of people wanting to hire motor cruisers instead of yachts this fact did not seem to affect Hunter's Fleet. Over the years the Yard had established a reputation for hiring out high quality yachts so they continued to attract enthusiastic yachtsmen who would never dream of hiring a motor cruiser. This fact, coupled with Percy's

Despite bowing to pressure from Blakes, Percy Hunter would not allow the recently acquired motor cruiser *Saskia* to be in the dyke on the same day as his yachts so she could only be hired from Wednesday to Wednesday! via Jim Searle

clear dislike for such craft, which he referred to simply as "stink boats", meant that it was highly unlikely that he would ever agree to these repeated requests. However, the unthinkable happened in 1962 when the motor cruiser *Saskia* joined Hunter's Fleet. She was built in the early 1950s by Collins Pleasure Craft at Oulton Broad for Mr de Carle Smith to tow his half decker *Priscilla* around the Broads. *Priscilla* was one of three half deckers built by the Hunters for private customers before the Second World War and was built to the same design as the two Woodcuts. Despite this apparent change in Percy's attitude *Saskia* was not

allowed to "pollute" the purity of his precious yachts so she could only be hired Wednesday to Wednesday to prevent her being in the dyke at the same time as the yachts!

Shortly before Christmas 1963 Percy became ill and, despite making a partial recovery, he died at his home across the road from his beloved boatyard on 26 January 1964. Percy's death was a major blow not just personally, but also professionally, for his sons. Although they tried to carry on with the business, the next couple of years became an increasing struggle for the Hunter brothers.

Norfolk County Council's Chief Education Officer between 1950 and 1974 was Dr (later Sir Lincoln) Ralphs. During his time in office, Sir Lincoln Ralphs was responsible for Norfolk County Council acquiring a number of outdoor facilities, such as Hunter's Fleet, to provide Norfolk's school children with a rounded education.

Photograph taken by Mr Johnson Taylor of Elm Hill Studio, via Lady Ralphs

Hustler 2 on the River Bure close to Thurne Mouth.

Chapter Three

The County's Fleet

The Norfolk County Sailing Base 1968 - 1996

As the Hunter brothers began their third letting season without Percy at the helm, the Fleet was about to face the biggest threat to its existence since the outbreak of the Second World War. The combination of Stanley's failing health, the absence of Percy's leadership and Cyril's desire to reduce his work load left the brothers with little choice but to put the Fleet up for sale in 1966. Those final years of family ownership had been an uphill struggle but the brothers were worried about the future of the business they had worked so hard together with their father to build up. They feared that the Fleet would be purchased by someone who would rebuild the yard and either modernise the boats or replace them with motor cruisers. How

73

However, Lady Luck seemed to be smiling on the Fleet because its appearance on the market coincided with Norfolk County Council's (NCC) quest to establish a sailing base to be used by Norfolk's school children.

Sailing was actively supported within Norfolk's schools by the county's Chief Education Officer, Dr Lincoln Ralphs (later Sir Lincoln Ralphs), who believed in the role of sailing as part of a child's overall education. He advocated that education should not be confined to the classroom because extra curricular activities, such as sailing, were an effective method of teaching children important "life skills", such as discipline, tolerance and team work. When asked to explain his philosophy of education Dr Ralphs once replied, "the purpose of education is to turn 'I cannot ' into 'I can.'" Sailing played an important role in this philosophy because handling a sailing boat requires a child to develop courage and responsibility. To put these views into action Dr Ralphs encouraged every school to provide dinghies for the use of their pupils, by either purchasing a complete Wayfarer dinghy, or building a Bittern dinghy from a kit under the supervision of the wood working teacher.

At a county level a sailing base was established on Filby Broad in the early 1960s to offer sailing courses for Norfolk school children, using the Education Authority's growing fleet of Wayfarer and Bittern dinghies. This amenity enabled the youngsters to learn the basics of sailing in a safe environment. However, it soon became apparent that there was a requirement for a sailing facility that had direct access to the main Broadland river network, thus catering for the needs of experienced students and equipping them with a wider set of skills than was possible within the confines of Filby Broad. This requirement coincided with the Education Authority's desire to create a centre for field studies so that students could study the natural environment of the Broads. Discussions soon turned towards the possibility of building a single facility that catered for both needs.

In 1964 NCC's Fleet Warden, Les Gee, and a local teacher, George Southgate, who is the son of the well known Horning-based boatbuilder Dick Southgate, were invited to draw up a short list of potential sites for the dual purpose centre. To ensure that each place on their list was suitable for both roles, the pair surveyed every site from the water and by foot. Their work revealed that a 5 acre site at Acle was the best option for further consideration by NCC. However, this plan was subsequently dropped, following a site inspection by representatives from both the Planning Department and the Education Authority, so a new list of sites had to be prepared which was also later blocked by the Planning Department. Frustrated by this lack of progress Dr Ralphs challenged the Planning Department to put forward their own suggestion, which led to the proposal to build the facilities at Stokesby. The Education Authority turned down this idea because the waters of the River Bure below Stokesby are an entirely unsuitable environment, in which to teach sailing, while the proposed location of the centre next to the pub was inappropriate.

While he tried to find a way to break the deadlock at the beginning of 1966 Dr Ralphs learnt that Hunter's Yard was about to be placed on the market and How Hill was going to be sold by public auction on 18 June. Neither option,

on its own, would solve the Council's requirement for a dual purpose centre but, between them, the two properties had the potential to fulfil the Council's needs. The Education Committee's Buildings & Sites Sub Committee agreed with this assessment and authorised the start of negotiations to purchase both sites on 11 June 1966.

With its varied collection of gardens and large house, How Hill seemed to offer the basis for an excellent field studies centre right in the heart of the Norfolk Broads. The 344 acre estate had been progressively transformed from open marshland by the prominent Norfolk architect Edward T Boardman and his wife Florence. They bought How Hill in 1902 as a result of problems with the booking arrangements for their sailing holiday. The couple had been due to spend a week sailing around the Broads onboard the pleasure wherry *Gaviota* but, when they travelled to Wroxham to begin their cruise, they discovered that the wherry was already out on hire. Rather than abandon their holiday plans, the Boardmans decided to charter the smaller *John Henry* instead. Unlike *Gaviota*, *John Henry* was able

Cyril Hunter at the helm of *Luna*.
© Peter Hollingham / NCC

to pass under the old Ludham Bridge thus enabling the Boardmans to explore the relatively narrow and twisty reed lined River Ant. As *John Henry* sailed towards Barton Broad the young couple caught their first glimpse of How Hill and immediately fell in love with the area. To the untrained eye the land at How Hill was simply open marshland, but Edward Boardman could see the potential of the site with its commanding views of the Ant Valley. The Boardmans bought the land soon after their return from the cruise onboard *John Henry* and, the following year, they began work on the large thatched house which was completed in 1904. By 1939 the

couple had created a series of gardens and planted more than 70,000 trees. Not surprisingly, the sale of such a well-placed property generated an enormous amount of interest. On the day of the sale the auction room in Norwich was packed, leading to some intense bidding, but the Education Authority won the day to secure the estate for £37,000.

Having secured How Hill, Dr Ralphs could concentrate upon the negotiations with the Hunter brothers to purchase Hunter's Yard. Without the pressure of an auctioneer's hammer, this process was conducted at a more leisurely pace. By May 1967 Dr Ralphs had reached an outline agreement with the Hunter brothers so that he could bring the issue before the Education Committee for approval at their July meeting. Although the Committee members were enthusiastic about the project they requested further information for their next meeting, thus introducing a further 2 month delay to the process. When the Committee discussed the issue again at their next meeting, on 9 September, Mr C.A. Pitt Steele was the only member to vote against the decision to purchase the Fleet for £35,000. However, the Educa-

This aerial shot clearly shows the layout of Hunter's Yard. The small dyke by the entrance to the Yard was excavated after the Second World War so that the Hunters could make some additional money by hiring out private moorings.

tion Authority could not complete the deal, until it had been formally ratified by the County Council at their next meeting on 7 October 1967. In its request for endorsement from the Council the Education Committee stated, "In making this recommendation we have been fully aware of the need to exercise appropriate financial restraints; the expenditure is well within the estimates provided for this type of development. We believe the opportunity for acquiring a site so well suited to our needs, and so advantageously located, is not likely to recur." Mr Pitt Steele led the opposition to this measure claiming that the money should be spent on repairs to school buildings. The Chairman of the Education Committee, Dr Harold Hudson, pointed out that the funds being used to purchase the Fleet had been specifically allocated for that type of activity and could not be used for maintaining buildings. Although Mr Pitt Steele and others continued to voice their

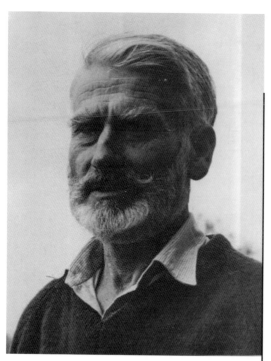

Following Hunter's Yard purchase by Norfolk County Council Cyril Hunter stayed on as a consultant and part time boatbuilder.   via Jennifer Mack

concerns in the local press the Council agreed by a majority of 15 votes to go ahead with the purchase of the Fleet.

With the documentation in place, NCC formally became the new owners of Hunter's Fleet on 1 January 1968 and re-named the Yard The Norfolk County Sailing Base. Stanley Hunter went into retirement, while Cyril Hunter stayed on to act as a part time consultant and boatbuilder. The responsibility of managing the Fleet was given to NCC's Fleet Warden, Les Gee, who transferred his

headquarters from Wensum Lodge to Ludham. His new duties were to be carried out in addition to his existing work, which included the inspection of sailing within Norfolk's schools, and running sailing courses at Filby Sailing Base. The Council agreed, as part of the deal to purchase the Yard, to the Hunters' request for yard hands Tom Grapes and Roger Nudd to be retained, while Miss McCully was recruited as the Yard's first Administrator. Miss McCully stayed only a short while at the Yard before she was succeeded by Josie Webb.

The change of ownership was a relatively low key affair with only minor coverage in the local press but, as the news reached Norfolk's schools, it was greeted with delight by many of the teachers. They were quick to appreciate that the Fleet provided them with the opportunity to take parties of school children for longer periods afloat than was possible at the Filby Sailing Base and that spending time onboard these boats would be so much more than a simple sailing holi-day. On a personal level the students would have to learn to live and work with their con-temporaries in a confined envi-

Above: A school party prepare to leave Hunter's Yard onboard *Hustler*.

Below: The basic nature of the Hunter yachts means that school children have to learn to work as a team if they are to successfully tackle tasks such as quanting.

Luna "shooting" the notorious Medieval bridge at Potter Heigham.
© Richard Johnstone-Bryden

ronment. Experience would also show that these courses helped to bring the students and teachers together in a way that was not otherwise possible. The lack of an engine onboard the yachts and half deckers meant that the students would have to work together as a team, and use the elements to their advantage, to sail the boats from A to B. At the same time, the students would begin to learn about the unique environment of the Broads. For many pupils, even those who attended schools by the various Broad-land rivers, such trips provided them with their first opportunity to experience the wonders of the Broads for themselves. When one thinks about the ge-

ography of the area it is hardly surprising because there are large parts of the network that are only accessible either from private land or by boat.

As the process of incorporating the Yard into the education system got underway, it looked as though the existing customers had sailed a Hunter yacht for the last time. With the exception of the customers who had already booked holidays before the end of June 1968 the Council would only take bookings from schools in Norfolk. However, detailed examination of how the schools would use the Fleet revealed that there would inevitably be periods within the sailing season when they could not make use of the

Fleet because of their other commitments such as exams. It seemed ridiculous to allow the boats to stay alongside in the Yard when they could be hired out to some of the Fleet's existing customers who were prepared to pay normal commercial rates. Therefore, a new system was introduced whereby Norfolk schools had priority over all other hirers. Once the Norfolk schools had confirmed their requirements for the season the Yard could sell off all remaining capacity at full commercial rates, compared to the 50% discount awarded to Norfolk school children. By taking this approach the Council had the added benefit of being able to raise some much needed revenue towards the cost of maintaining the Fleet. The only disadvantage for some of the existing customers was that their bookings were not confirmed until shortly before their holiday in case a Norfolk school wanted to book a trip. Despite this uncertainty, many of the long term customers continued to book their holidays with the Yard, such as Dikky Dale who first hired a Hustler in 1954. Following his retirement, Dikky ended up spending much of the summer cruising the Broads single handed in

Hustler 2, until his death in October 1998. When he was asked why he didn't buy his own Broads yacht Dikky replied by saying that *Hustler 2* was not for sale!

Another aspect of the existing customer base that continued to use the Fleet were a number of associations. Of these The Bitter Boys have the honour of being the longest running customer of the Fleet. The group was founded in 1926, when some members of the Lloyds Bank Rugby Club decided to form an association for those who wanted to learn how to sail. For their early Broadland holidays they hired yachts from G. Smith's yard in Wroxham, before enlarging their "fleet" and becoming one of the first customers of Percy Hunter & Sons in 1932. The group earned their distinctive name because when they started coming to Norfolk they brought their own bitter - Broadland pubs only sold mild beer. The first "Admiral" of the Bitter Boys was Ken Roberts who developed a deep love for the Norfolk Broads and subsequently retired there to spend the summer months onboard his yacht *Kittywake*. Ken was a lifelong bachelor so when *Kittywake* was out of the water he would stay either at Hickling's Pleasure Boat or Broads Haven at Potter Heigham. When he died in 1974 John Cole was appointed as his successor.

The group operates a fairly laid back programme which has remained virtually unaltered throughout the years. A designated skipper and cook is allocated to each boat and payment is based on the kitty system, i.e. all hire charges, breakages and beer are shared between those present. The size of every cruise is decided during the preceding December when the members attend the Bitter Boy's annual Christmas party in London, with the composition of each crew agreed at a subsequent meeting in April. Every day of their cruise is split into two phases, with a stop at a Broads pub for lunch, and then another one for the night. The destinations are chosen by the "Admiral" according to the prevailing conditions to give the crews enough time to enjoy a drink before their meal! The passage between pubs is not a race, so the boats set off from the moorings when they are ready and make their way to the next rendezvous at their own pace. About the only aspect of the Bitter Boys to have changed is that the scope of their membership has increased to include sons and grandsons of the old stalwarts.

Like the Bitter Boys, youth groups, such as the Scouts and the Scripture Union began in the late 1960s to increasingly switch over to hiring yachts from Hunter's Fleet. Although the activities of Scout groups receive a fair amount of publicity the work of Christian groups has gone largely unnoticed, despite the major contribution they make to introducing young people to Broadland sailing. Christian groups first started bringing parties of young people to the Broads in the 1920s following a meeting of Chaplains from some of the nation's most important public schools who thought that their pupils would benefit from such a cruise. Nearly 80 years later these groups are still organising Broadland cruises each summer and introduce between 600 - 800 young people to Broads sailing every year.

To underline his support for the County Sailing Base the Chairman of the Education Committee, Dr Harold Hudson, donated his half decker *Brown Bess* to the Council to become part of Hunter's Fleet. He had been unable to use her for a few years so he thought that she could be put to better use alongside the two Woodcuts. *Brown Bess* was built by Percivals in Horning as one of six gunter rigged Middle Nene One Designs on speculation for the Middle Nene Sailing Club. The half decker was originally fitted with auxiliary power in the form of a small Stuart Turner engine which was subsequently removed. During her time ashore *Brown Bess* had dried out so when she was re-launched by Percivals for the short passage to Ludham four oil drums were strapped to each side to provide additional buoyancy as a precaution. On arrival *Brown Bess* was slipped so that Cyril Hunter could fully access her condition. He found that her hull planking was generally sound but her keel and many of her timbers were in need of replacement. It was also decided to take the opportunity to replace her gunter rig with a balanced lug sail rig in the interests of commonality of spares with the pair of Woodcuts.

During the winter of 1969 the trading wherry *Lord Roberts* arrived at the Yard as part of the preparations for the proposed Museum of the Broads which was planned to be built by the Education Authority on the marshland alongside the

Brown Bess on the River Bure with Wisemans Mill, Oby in the background.
© Peter Hollingham / NCC

Yard where the Broads Authority Field Base now stands. The idea of establishing the Museum was mooted in 1968 by a small group led by the broadcaster and local teacher Dick Bagnall-Oakley. As part of their plans they wanted to preserve an example of a trading wherry, pleasure wherry and a wherry yacht as well as artefacts, photographs, documents and oral accounts from those who lived and worked on the Broads. The Museum would principally cater for children from primary and secondary schools who would be brought to Ludham by water using a pleasure cruiser from Broads Tours which had agreed to offer a discount to school parties. While the Education Authority waited for the go-ahead from the planning department Les Gee received an offer from the Norfolk Wherry Trust to donate *Lord Roberts* to the Museum as the representative trading wherry. The timing of this proposal was ideal for the Trust which had been trying to decide what to do with *Lord Roberts* since she was donated by May Gurney in May 1969. The future of *Lord Roberts* had presented a major problem to all involved since May Gurney decided that they would not fund the major refit that was required to keep her operational. Despite their decision the company felt that it could not simply break up the last commercially operated Norfolk Wherry so they approached the Trust to see if they wanted to operate her alongside *Albion*. The Trust did not want to be seen to refuse the opportunity of preserving *Lord Roberts* but they did not have the funds to restore her either. The Harbour Master at Oulton Broad offered to help by providing a mooring for *Lord Roberts* while the Trust decided what to do with her. As the months passed, without any ap-

parent progress, the Harbour Master grew increasingly concerned about her deteriorating condition, before finally asking the Trust to move her elsewhere. Sympathising with the Trust's situation Les Gee agreed to allow the Trust to moor *Lord Roberts* at the Yard in the expectation that the plans for the Museum would be given the go-ahead and that she would join the collection. However, the Planning Department's decision to turn down the proposal for the Museum left the Trust and NCC in an awkward position so Les Gee agreed to allow *Lord Roberts* to remain in the cross dyke at the top of the Yard until an alternative home could be found for her. Unfortunately, the Harbour Master's fears proved to be entirely justified because, within a year of her arrival in Ludham, *Lord Roberts* sank. On 9 June 1974 a party of firemen from both the Stalham Fire Brigade and Great Yarmouth Fire Brigade raised the wherry as a joint training exercise. When she was brought to the surface the firemen hosed her down only to find that she was full of eels which they caught by chasing after them around the vast empty hull with buckets! Within a fortnight *Lord Roberts*

Above: *Lord Roberts* is brought to the surface by a team of firemen from the Great Yarmouth and Stalham Fire Brigades as an exercise on 9 June 1974.   Both photographs © Jim Searle

Below: The fireman are hosing down the vast open hold of *Lord Roberts*.

The final resting place of the trading wherry *Lord Roberts* in a private dyke in Hoveton.

Both photographs © Richard Johnstone-Bryden

Wherry yacht *Olive* on Oulton Broad.

sank again and remained on the bottom until 1983 when she was raised again and towed to Hoveton, where she subsequently sank in a private dyke.

After two successful seasons at the helm of the Fleet, Les Gee resigned as NCC's Fleet Warden in 1970 to take up a new appointment in the Lake District. By the time of his departure sailing was a firmly established part of life within Norfolk's schools. In addition to Hunter's Fleet the Education Authority owned ten Wayfarers, eighteen Bitterns, six 12ft clinker boats, known as Norwich Amateur Rowing Club One Designs, and the various schools owned approximately 190 boats between them. Jim Searle was selected as Les Gee's successor and, shortly afterwards, the Yard gained a full time boatbuilder when Graham Cooper was appointed to the staff.

When the Council purchased Hunter's Fleet they retained the small motor cruiser *Saskia* but she never really fitted in with the new role of the Fleet. She was initially used as a support boat for the half deckers during sailing courses. Unfortunately, her limited speed proved to be a handicap because, in a good breeze, the half

The Waveney One Design *Sundew* became the fourth half decker within Hunter's Fleet when she was donated to NCC in 1973 by Richard Sanders.
© Richard Johnstone-Bryden

deckers usually sailed off into the distance and then had to wait for *Saskia* to arrive with the hot drinks etc. In the end it was decided to take packed lunches onboard the half deckers and *Saskia* was eventually sold by the Council in 1977. However, the opportunity to acquire a more effective support boat arose in 1973 when the owner of the 58ft wherry yacht *Olive* offered to sell her to the Council. Although it would not have been possible to slip her at the Yard she would have provided another dimension to the range of sail training offered by the County Sailing Base, as well as adding prestige to the Fleet. Sadly, the Council were not prepared to fund such an ambitious project and she was purchased by her present owner Peter Bower a year later.

Despite the Council's reluctance to buy *Olive* in 1973 there were nonetheless changes to the composition of the Fleet that year. Firstly, the Waveney One Design (WOD) *Sundew* was donated by Richard Sanders to bring the number of half deckers up to four boats. The gunter rigged WODs were designed by the Oulton Broad shipwright William Parker, in response to the Waveney Sailing Club's request for a new One Design class to be raced by their members. Between 1922 and 1955 twenty-six wooden WODs were built, with the first batch of six completed by the Evans yard at Kirkley, Suffolk. Today, the Class is experiencing a period of further expansion with the building of new GRP WODs. WODs are often mistaken by the untrained eye for the more numerous Yare & Bure One Designs (Y&BOD) which are perhaps better known as white boats. The easiest way to tell the two classes apart when they are sailing is by the red W prefix and sail numbers

as opposed to the black numbers on the sail of the Y&BOD. Other differences between the two classes include the WODs possessing a more substantial construction to cope with the rougher conditions encountered on the southern rivers, while the Y&BODs have a single shroud each side as opposed to two shrouds on the WOD. The Y&BODs also carry a horse on the aft deck and a bow buoyancy tank which can be entered via a hatch on the foredeck. *Sundew* was built in 1951, by Jack Fowler in his boat shed at the end of his garden in Lowestoft, for F Henderson. Three years later she was sold to W Sanders and remained within the Sanders family until she was donated to the Council.

The second change to the Fleet in 1973 occurred as a result of a serious accident in the Yard towards the end of the season. Having spent the last night of their holiday onboard *Woodruff* at the Yard, her hirers lit the gas stove for their breakfast. Unbeknown to them the bilges had been filling up overnight with gas so, a split second after they struck the match, *Woodruff* was rocked by a gas explosion which ripped through the boat, splitting every plank down to the waterline and dis-

Above: As part of her rebuild in the 1970s *Woodruff* was fitted with a bowsprit as can be clearly seen in this view of her ashore.

Both photographs © Celia and Fred Belbin, (via Ron and Lesley Bonshor)

Right: *Woodruff* as she is today on the River Bure at Horning.

The Yachting World Bass Boat on Filby Broad shortly after she was built by Graham Cooper at Hunter's Yard. © Peter Hollingham / NCC

lodging the transom and bulkheads. About the only items holding her together were the cabin sides, otherwise she would have sunk. Amid this scene of utter devastation the oil lamp glass remained intact in its normal position! Unbelievably, the hirers managed to walk away without any serious injuries. It is believed that the hirers broke the gas tap during the course of their holiday, so they weren't entirely sure whether the gas was switched on or off. *Woodruff* was subsequently slipped for a thorough inspection and written off by the insurance company. The Yard declined the insurance company's offer to buy back the wreck because she would have required a complete rebuild which the Council was unwilling to fund. Therefore, *Woodruff* was sold by sealed tender to Neil Hunt who refitted her at Acle. As part of the work carried out at Acle, provision was made for an outboard engine and she was given a gaff topsail rig complete with bowsprit. Today, *Woodruff* is still a familiar sight on the Broads and has been owned since September 1980 by Lesley and Ron Bonshor, who occasionally bring *Woodruff* back to her former home for special events.

During the 1970s the

Yard progressively took on the responsibility for maintaining the Council's fleet of wooden Wayfarer dinghies used at the Filby Sailing Base. Once Hunter's Fleet had been re-launched at the beginning of each season the staff at the Yard turned their attention to refitting the Wayfarers. As part of this added responsibility Graham Cooper built the Bass Boat in 1978 for use by the Council as a rescue boat on Filby Broad. As she was nearing completion someone re-marked that her outboard well resembled a commode so Jim Searle decided to register her with the Great Yarmouth Port and Haven Commissioners as *Commodious*! When the Bass Boat was eventually replaced by a high speed dory at Filby, she was allocated to the Yard for use as a support boat for the Fleet at Ludham. History re-peated itself when the Bass Boat was withdrawn from ser-vice by the Yard in 2003 and replaced by a high speed dory.

By the early 1980s there had been a distinct shift in em-phasis in Norfolk's education policies. The days of Dr Ralphs' wider vision when great importance was attached to a child's overall education had passed. A new era of budget-led policies had arrived, threatening to undermine some of the achievements of Dr Ralphs and those who had sup-ported him during his time as the County's Chief Education Officer. As Margaret Thatcher's first Government tried to bring public spending under control the effects began to be felt in Norfolk as the County Council looked for ways to reduce its budgets in line with Government policy in 1981. As part of this review the Education Committee ap-pointed Mrs Frances Roualle as the leader of a new Working Group to investigate the work of its extra curricular facilities, including the County Sailing Base. It was clear that there was a very high probability that one of the facilities was going to be closed, so those behind each centre had to present a strong case for their retention by the Council.

When the Education Committee held its annual dis-cussion in January 1982 to set the hire charges for the coming season they advised the Yard to only take bookings on a provi-sional basis for the 1982 season until the findings of the Work-ing Group were known. This, coupled with comments from Mrs Roualle in the press where

Lullaby starred in the BBC's adaptation of Arthur Ransome's Coot Club and Big Six as the fictitious *Teasel.* © Richard Johnstone-Bryden

she appeared to be advocating the concentration of sailing resources at one location and the use of modern dinghies in preference to the old Ludham-based boats, led the Yard's supporters, including The Norfolk Schools Sailing Association, to fear the worst. Their Commodore, Mr Christopher Webb, who was a teacher at Stalham High School, fired the opening shots in the battle to prevent the sale by saying, "We've had tremendous results from there over the years, with people going through to the Olympic and national teams. It would be a tragedy if they were to kick it away from underneath us now, when we've been running it on such a tight budget." Meanwhile the Association's Secretary, Mr Colin Brown, was equally quick to dispel any suggestions that the boats were worn out and in need of replacement.

When the Working Group finally visited the Yard on 7 April 1982 the first signs of a retreat began to appear when Mrs Roualle conceded, "I believe we may have had some misinformation in the past about there being very old boats here, and about just how many schools use them. But at Filby, for instance, we learnt that lots of associations we had never even heard about use the place." The campaign to save the Yard received further public support from the national coach of the Royal Yachting Association, John Driscoll, who said, "There are very few opportunities for training in the area, particularly as Norfolk is a rural county with a low density population. The Broads have been a breeding ground for yachtsmen for generations and it would be a disaster for any one of the few centres to close especially as they are doing such tremendous work for young people."

The campaign to save the Yard soon gathered momentum, both behind the scenes and in public, leading to the Education Authority ultimately granting the Yard a stay of execution while it switched its attention to How Hill. Like Hunter's Fleet, the issue of disposing of the County Field Studies Centre at How Hill became a controversial subject as local people expressed their strong support for its retention. Sadly, there was to be no reprieve for How Hill and the following year NCC announced that Norwich Union Insurance Group were going to buy How Hill House for £120,000 and the Broads Authority would purchase the 344 acre estate for £120,000. However, this was not the end of How Hill's contribution to the education of young people because The How Hill Trust was formed to continue the work of How Hill. A 99 year lease was agreed between the Trust and

Norwich Union while the Broads Authority agreed to grant the Trust rights of access to parts of the estate. In a further act of generosity Norwich Union handed over the Deeds for How Hill House to the Trust on 19 April 2002. To safeguard the future of both the building and the services provided by the Trust it launched an appeal for £450,000 to mark the centenary of the house's completion. At the time of writing the Trust had already raised £300,000 towards its target.

After an eventful year for the staff at Ludham, life appeared to be returning to normal as the routine work of slipping and maintaining the Fleet got underway in October 1982. That winter the Yard received a telephone call from the BBC about their intention to produce Arthur Ransome's stories Coot Club and Big Six for television. The BBC needed to find an authentic 1930s style Broads yacht to use as *Teasel* and wondered if it would be possible to hire one of the Hunter yachts for the duration of the filming, which was expected to last about three months. When the researcher visited the Yard he decided that they wanted to use *Lullaby,* which had been stripped back to bare wood and

While *Lullaby* starred, *Lustre* (seen here on the River Thurne) and the rest of the Fleet were hard at work as usual.

© Richard Johnstone-Bryden

was about to be re-varnished. Once a deal had been reached between the BBC and the Council the preparations for her new role began with the replacement of her Tracmark decks with traditional brown linoleum and the application of the name *Teasel* on the transom. For the first half of the season her stage name was covered up with a neat little name board that was removed prior to her handover to the BBC at the end of June. At the same time

her modern synthetic ropes were exchanged for hemp and her Terylene sails were replaced by a suit of Duradon sails to ensure that she looked as authentic as possible. Although the Duradon sails looked like cotton sails they proved to be too heavy for the spars and caused several cracks in them during filming.

In addition to the long term hire of *Lullaby,* the Yard also benefited from various jobs in the lead up to the start of filming, such as completing the conversion of a former ship's lifeboat into *Death & Glory.* Unfortunately, the team from the BBC Props Department had not worked on boats before so they had not considered the effects that their work would have on the lifeboat's stability. By the time they had finished their work *Death & Glory* was in great danger of living up to her name! Ian Grapes, who had only been at the Yard for two seasons, sorted out the problems by rebuilding the cabin using lighter wood so that *Death & Glory* could be used without drowning the actors. Another task involved the conversion of an 11ft varnished dinghy from the Fleet into *Titmouse* and the cleaning up of an old punt built

Above & Below: The new *Brown Bess* begins to take shape in 1987 in the "building berth" where most of the Fleet were built.

Both photographs © Jim Searle

Graham Cooper working on the new *Brown Bess*.

The planking on the new *Brown Bess* is complete.

Above: Ian Grapes at the helm of *Hustler 2*

All colour photographs © Richard Johnstone-Bryden

PLATE IX

Above: Paul Bowen replaces one of *Rebel Reveller's* planks during her restoration.

Below: Simon Crudgington extracts a steamed timber from the Yard's steam box during *Rebel Reveller's* restoration.

PLATE X

Above: Ian Grapes at the helm of *Rebel Reveller* on the River Bure

Below: *Wood Violet* at the end of another winter overhaul

PLATE XI

Above: Graham Cooper at work on the new 4 berth yacht

Below: The new 4 berth yacht begins to take on a recognisable shape.

PLATE XII

Above: (left to right) *Sundew*, *Brown Bess* and *Hustler* on the River Bure

Below:Quant power! *Lullaby* emerges from the notorious Medieval bridge at Potter Heigham

PLATE XIII

Above: None of the Hunter yachts have an engine so when the wind dies or the mast has to be lowered for a bridge the only alternative form of power is provided by the quant pole.

PLATE XIV

Above: Reflections

Below: Waiting for the slip

PLATE XV

Above: Once each yacht is slipped it is cleaned below the waterline with a power washer and scrubbing brush before it is moved into its winter berth within the shed.

Below: A perfect breeze.

PLATE XVI

Above: From the stern quarter, the planking on the new *Brown Bess* is nearly complete.

© Jim Searle

Right: The new *Brown Bess* completed and sailing by Thurne Mouth.

© Richard Johnstone-Bryden

by Cyril Hunter. The Yard was given a cameo role as the fictitious Wroxham boatyard of Rodley & Co where the motor cruiser *Margoletta* was repaired following her accident at the notorious Medieval bridge at Potter Heigham. Not surprisingly, the Yard needed little preparation before filming could begin, apart from the application of a fresh coat of creosote and the temporary replacement of the Norfolk County Sailing Base sign with one for Rodley & Co. The filming itself was straightforward but there were a few problems when the staff tried to re-launch *Margoletta* because the tide had dropped so much.

Meanwhile, *Lullaby's* three months with the BBC took her all over the Broads, including a week on Breydon Water to film the scene depicting the grounding of *Teasel*. This involved mooring *Lullaby* each day in Ship Drain and laying four anchors that would not be seen! Filming onboard *Lullaby* was quite challenging for the BBC because there was only enough room for the actors and the essential film crew. The rest of the production staff were left on the support, boat or deployed on other boats to keep the holidaymakers out of the way when the film crew were shooting scenes.

The Fleet's involvement with the BBC was a tremendous windfall, which was to bring both short and long term benefits for the Yard. In addition to the income generated by the filming itself, such as the charter fee for *Lullaby,* the subsequent broadcast of the programmes created enormous interest in the Fleet to the point where parents would bring their children to see "Rodley & Co", "Teasel" and "Titmouse." One family took things a step further and hired *Lullaby* for a number of years afterwards, complete with *Titmouse* in which their son would sleep every night, to live out the Coot Club and Big Six stories. To capitalise on this interest *Lullaby* continued to be known by her stage name of *Teasel* until her transom had to be replaced at the end of the following season. Rather than burn this small piece of TV history the transom was erected within the shed as a lasting memorial to *Lullaby's* film role. The first two series should have been followed by the making of "We Didn't Mean To Go To Sea". Unfortunately, these programmes fell victim to the BBC's decision to concentrate on making more contemporary programmes because it had produced far too many costume dramas!

The Yard's next major project occurred in 1986 when it was decided to withdraw *Brown Bess* from the Fleet. Although she had been given an extensive refit in 1968, when she was donated to the Council, she was now in a very poor condition and in need of a complete rebuild. Rather than waste a lot of time trying to incorporate a few original timbers into the restoration work it was decided to use the old hull as a pattern and build a new boat to the original design. Therefore, the only items that were transferred from the old boat were the keel and the rig which had been added in 1968. Because of the high workload at the Yard in the winter the building work was confined to the summer months. Appropriately enough, Dr Hudson was invited to perform the launching ceremony in May 1988 shortly before the new *Brown Bess* joined the Fleet. Inspired by the success of this project, Jim Searle tried to persuade the Council to back the building of a new yacht to an original Hunter design but they were not prepared to allocate the necessary funding.

Throughout the early 1990s there were clear signs that the Council's long term commitment to the Fleet was becoming much weaker. As the Education Budget continued to come under increasing pressure, the Council tried to cut corners and reduced the amount of money it spent on maintaining both the Yard and the boats. The clearest sign of this trend came in October 1994 when Tom Grapes finally retired from the Yard after 47 years of continuous service. Although there was an obvious need for someone to replace Tom, the Council were not prepared to appoint a successor, thus leaving just Graham Cooper and Ian Grapes as the only full time members of the maintenance team. Thankfully, Tom could not resist the pull of the Yard and within a fortnight of retiring he agreed to come back to work on a part time basis to provide some much needed assistance with the winter maintenance programme. This, coupled with the high standards of the boats, meant that the Fleet was not seriously affected by the drop in manpower that winter. Fortunately, external events were about to change everything at the Yard and herald a period of renewed interest in the Fleet.

The colours of the Hunter family fly proudly over "their" yard again.
© Richard Johnstone-Bryden

This evocative shot of Hunter's Fleet was used on the front page of the Eastern Daily Press when the newspaper broke the story of Norfolk County Council's decision to sell Hunter's Fleet in 1995.

© Jim Searle

Chapter Four

The Bombshell

The Disposal & Subsequent Preservation Of Hunter's Fleet

Behind closed doors within County Hall the members of NCC's Education Committee held secret discussions to review the future of Hunter's Fleet on 18 January 1995, as part of their drive to identify possible economy measures to reduce their budget. At the end of their debate the members of the Committee agreed to explore the options for disposing of the Yard and its fleet, thereby creating the real risk that this unique collection of veteran Broadland sailing craft would be dispersed.

Of course it was not the first time that the future of the Fleet had been placed in doubt, since it was acquired by NCC in 1968. Whenever the Council needed to find savings within the Education Budget, the Fleet was seen by some as an easy target. Previously, the issue had been side stepped because many councillors were worried that the negative public reaction to such an announcement

Some of the Fleet at Thurne Dyke.

© Richard Johnstone-Bryden

would greatly outweigh the limited financial gains. However, critics of the Fleet thought that the facts could now play into their hands, not least that the numbers of Norfolk schools using the Fleet had dropped to an all time low of just two schools during the 1994 season. Such disappointing figures provided easy ammunition for those who wanted to use the issue to further their own political agenda. As the subsequent media campaign unfolded it became clear that some councillors saw the disposal of the Fleet as a useful pawn in their game of political brinkmanship with the Government in the run up to a General Election. Such individuals hoped that the local population would sympathise with them for having to take a courageous decision in difficult times, whilst at the same time blaming the Government for the Council's predicament, which had forced them to jeopardise the future of an important part of Norfolk's heritage. The clearest indication of this hidden agenda was provided when the Eastern Daily Press (EDP) published a letter from the Chairman of the Education Committee, Dr George Turner. Within this letter Dr Turner attempted to justify the Committee's plans and tried to shift the blame for the decision directly on to the Government three times. However, the proposed disposal of the Fleet was to prove a serious political miscalculation.

An advert within the EDP provided the only public announcement of the Education Committee's controversial decision, when Norfolk Property Services invited offers for the Fleet by Monday 27 March 1995. Picking up on the advert, the newspaper's editorial team requested permission for one of their reporters to have access to the Yard and interview the staff. The Council agreed to the request but failed to send a representative from County Hall to supervise the encounter, leaving the staff with an interesting dilemma. Although the Council was about to make all of them redundant, they were still employees of the Council who believed that they were expected to publicly back the policies of their employers. However, the Council's failure to provide a representative gave the staff an opportunity to present the case for saving the Yard. Lisa Morgan had been appointed as Josie Webb's successor on a six month contract shortly before the crisis broke. In the brief period since the start of her new

job, Lisa had become convinced of the Yard's importance as a key part of Norfolk's heritage. She strongly believed that if humanly possible a campaign should be instigated to save the Yard, but she was also conscious that such moves could run the risk of incurring serious consequences for either Tom, Graham or Ian. This was an important consideration because there was a remote possibility that the Council would withdraw the Yard from the market if it could not attract an acceptable bid. Therefore, as the member of staff with the least to lose, Lisa agreed to act as the person who would present the case for the preservation of the Fleet.

As a result of the subsequent interview, the EDP ran the story as its lead item on 23 February, which provoked an immediate response. Shocked by this news the people of Norfolk condemned the Council's decision and focused their anger directly towards Dr George Turner and his colleagues. Any hopes that some councillors may have had of being able to quietly dispose of Hunter's Fleet evaporated overnight as the EDP decided to represent the views it was receiving from many of its readers by launching the "Save Our Sailfleet" campaign. In the weeks that followed, the EDP kept the issue alive by featuring an interesting cross section of letters from people who passionately believed in the survival of the Fleet.

Meanwhile, at the Yard, the phone began to ring as concerned supporters of the Fleet rallied round to pledge their support, while others sent in donations, including one man who walked into the Yard and asked who he should make his cheque out to. This presented the staff with their next problem because in the flurry of activity that followed the publication of the first EDP feature no one had had the time to think about opening a bank account for the campaign. Equally, no one had considered what to call the group. Like any new organisation choosing the name can be quite difficult but the staff wanted the title to reflect the aims of the campaign, which resulted in the rather long winded "The Heritage Yacht Fleet Trust (Hunter's Yard)." Having resolved these issues, the staff had to move quickly if they were to gain the initiative. The strength of public opinion appeared to catch the Council off guard as they

maintained a low profile, while their staff at Ludham were effectively in open revolt against the Education Committee's plans.

Although they had gained an early advantage the staff needed to find the right people who could help them draw up a viable proposal to purchase the Yard. Without this help their campaign would quickly run out of momentum and end in failure. In a surprising twist the staff managed to arrange a meeting with NCC's County Education Officer, Michael Edwards, to discuss the situation and what they hoped to achieve. He appeared to be sympathetic to their objectives, but there was little he could actively do to support them. The only glimmer of hope that he could offer was that he did know someone who could lead this sort of project. Michael Edwards promised to discuss the situation with this person and, if he wanted to help, he would make direct contact with the Yard. Boosted by this pledge, the staff left County Hall a little happier but, as the days passed without any contact from this mystery person, their optimism started to ebb away as they began to wonder if all their efforts had been for nothing.

Fortunately, their fears proved to be unfounded because a few days later Lisa received a telephone call from Bryan Read, who identified himself as the person that Michael Edwards had mentioned. Although Bryan had never previously visited Hunter's Yard before, he has sailed on the Broads all of his life, and was a member of the Great Yarmouth Port and Haven Commission from 1963 to 1984. From 1977 to 1984 he chaired the Rivers Committee, which had responsibility for navigation on the Rivers and Broads of Norfolk and Suffolk. He was subsequently involved in the formation of the Broads Authority, on which he sat for 4 years. As a result of this experience he was well known to the Broads Authority's Chief Executive, Professor Aitken Clark, who contacted him about the same time as Michael Edwards in connection with the plight of Hunter's Yard. Despite the Authority's deep interest in the fate of the Fleet, Aitken Clark had concluded that it was not something that they could take on, so he was keen to encourage the formation of a Working Group that would be able to mount a credible bid.

In response to both of these requests, Bryan chaired a meeting on 1 March at the King Of Hearts art centre in Norwich to see who was interested in joining a Steering Group. As a result of this meeting the Norfolk Heritage Fleet Steering Group was formed, consisting of Bryan Read (Chairman), Professor Keith Clayton, Sam Hornor, Basil de Iongh, Leslie Mogford, Lisa Morgan, Paul Stevens, and Anthony Trafford. During the course of their research, the Steering Group found it quite hard to obtain accurate figures from the Council, while the Education Department proved to be thoroughly unhelpful because the disposal of the Yard was such a sensitive issue. However, there were elements within the Council who were very supportive of their work, especially within Norfolk Property Services which was responsible for its disposal. There were even those inside the Council who argued for the Yard's retention, but the Education Committee were determined to sell it, despite the Council's initial statements in February that is was merely exploring the possibility of selling the Fleet. As the media campaign unfolded Dr Turner admitted in the press that his Committee were considering,

While the future of the Fleet continued to be debated in the media the staff at the Yard had to carry on with their normal jobs and prepare the Fleet for another busy season. © Richard Johnstone-Bryden

how, rather than if, the sale would go ahead.

The public campaign to save the Fleet brought some early results when the Council was forced to make a few concessions, such as the extension of the deadline for proposals to allow bidders enough time to put together credible plans. Equally, the public outcry had increased the pressure on the Council to pay more attention to the bidders' long term plans for the Fleet, rather than simply concentrating on the amount of money they would be prepared to pay for the site and the boats. All of these developments played into the hands of the Steering Group as its members put together their bid. However, the Steering Group were faced with the major challenge of how to keep the media campaign alive because, after the initial burst of coverage, there would inevitably be a period of limbo, in which there would be little to report while the plans were being drawn up. Thankfully, the EDP's Deputy Editor, Martin Kirby, was a strong supporter of the Steering Group and managed to keep the "Save Our Sailfleet" campaign going. Meanwhile, back at the Yard, the staff still had their normal

Some of the Fleet approach the outskirts of the village of Potter Heigham as the first of the riverside bungalows loom into view.

© Richard Johnstone-Bryden

jobs to perform, not least to ensure that the Fleet was ready for the start of what was to prove an extremely busy season. Not only had all the media coverage galvanised public support for the preservation of the Fleet, but it had also led to an increase in bookings as more people wanted to sample the experience of sailing a Hunter yacht.

Within a couple of months of its formation the Steering Group had completed its bid. In a letter, dated 17 May 1995, to Norfolk Property Services the Steering Group set out its plans to purchase the Yard and its boats for £255,000. The key points of interest from the Steering Group's proposal included:

cluded:

1   If their offer was accepted an independent Trust with charitable status would be formed with Education in its widest sense as its main aim.

2   The Trust would give an undertaking that the Fleet would not be split up and that it would continue to operate from its Ludham base.

3   The Trust would continue to offer private moorings but the Trust would not seek to extend the moorings.

4   The Steering Group would form an endowment fund to support a preferential rate for the educational use of the boats by all Norfolk schools, including groups asso-

With a bone in her teeth *Hustler 5* charges down the River Thurne under full sail towards Thurne Mouth. © Richard Johnstone-Bryden

ciated with the Norfolk Youth and Community Service. A lower rate of subsidy might also be offered to youth groups from outside Norfolk.

5 The Trust would be committed to maintaining the necessary boat building skills needed to build and maintain wooden yachts. The Trust would look to establish an apprenticeship scheme. The Trust would also consider long term plans to increase the size of the Fleet and initiate a long term replacement programme for the Fleet when the existing boats reached the end of their working lives.

6 As part of the Millennium celebrations the Trust would build a new wooden yacht along similar lines to the existing yachts.

When the Council's final deadline for submissions expired, a total of six proposals had been sent in for evaluation. The merits of each bid were considered in secret by the Education Committee on 17 July. As a result of these deliberations, the Committee rejected four of the proposals, to leave a short list of the Steering Group and the Norfolk Broads Yachting Co (NBYCo). This decision in effect put the Steering Group in pole position, because NBYCo's Director, Mike Barnes, had already publicly stated, in an interview for the EDP, that NBYCo would give the Trust first refusal. Explaining their decision Mike Barnes remarked at the time, "The Trust appears to have gained the weight of public opinion. Normally, we would be interested but this time we will stand to one side and let them have first shot."

Having gained prime position, the Steering Group embarked on its mammoth task to raise £300,000, form the Norfolk Heritage Fleet Trust (NHFT) and obtain charitable status. From this point things moved quickly because the Council was keen to relinquish its responsibility for managing the Fleet as soon as possible. A month later the Trust had reached an agreement with the Council, whereby the Trust would pay a 10% deposit in April 1996, and take over responsibility for the Fleet during the 1996 Hire Season, while NCC would remain as the legal owner. The Trust would be required to pay the balance of the sale price at the end of the season, at which point the Trust would become the new owners of the Yard and its boats. The deal suited both sides because it removed any personal liability for the Trustees, whilst putting the Council in the clear pub-

licly. In the event of the Trust failing to raise the necessary funds, the Council could put the Fleet back on the market, whilst being able to claim that it had done everything possible to assist moves to preserve the Fleet.

To bring the Trust's plans to fruition they were hoping for a major grant from the National Lottery Heritage Lottery Fund. Being optimistic, the Trust initially applied for £140,000 because they felt confident that they could raise the balance from other sources. Having successfully negotiated their way through the early stages of the application process, one of the Heritage Lottery Fund Commissioners arranged to visit Ludham to see the Yard and its Fleet for herself in February 1996. The meeting was timed for lunchtime so Lisa asked Graham Cooper's wife Candy to prepare some sandwiches and her finest scones. In keeping with the theme of the visit Candy made a typical boat-builder's lunch with deep filled big cut sandwich's, much to Lisa's horror because she thought their visitors might be expecting a more sophisticated spread. However, Candy's menu was an inspired choice because when their guests saw the food they immediately cried

The Broadcaster Paul Heiney (left) with Bryan Read, the Chairman of Norfolk Heritage Fleet Trust .   via Bryan Read

out, "thank goodness no vol-au-vents!" Everyone thought that the visit was a big success, but there was to be an agonising wait before the Trust would know if their application was going to be approved.

As the hand over day approached the Trust started to think about some of the fine detail of how the Yard and boats would be presented. It was felt that the Norfolk County Sailing Base sign on the boatshed should be replaced. Although the Fleet would be operated by NHFT it was felt that it would be inconceivable for the Yard to be known by any other name than Hunter's Yard so it was

decided to paint Hunter's Yard in large letters with the name of the Trust in much smaller letters above. Equally, it was felt that the burgee created for the Norfolk County Sailing Base should be dropped in favour of the original Hunter's burgee.

On 1 April 1996, over 200 people gathered at the Yard to witness the Trust assume operational control of the Fleet. As part of the event the TV broadcaster and writer Paul Heiney was invited to formally launch the public appeal to raise £300,000 by hoisting the Hunter Burgee up the boatshed's flag pole. It was the first time since the early 1970s that

On completion of the festivities ashore to mark the day that the Trust assumed operational control of the Fleet, Paul Heiney was given the honour of having the first sail of the day.

© Richard Johnstone-Bryden

the red, white and blue Hunter burgee had been seen in Broadland waters. Throughout the day's festivities Bryan Read had to keep some momentous news to himself. A week before the launch Bryan had received a letter from the Heritage Lottery Fund confirming that the Trust would be awarded a substantial grant, providing they complied with a number of conditions. The letter then explained that the Heritage Lottery Fund felt that the Trust had not applied for enough money, so they had decided to award a grant of £200,000 instead of the £140,000 sum that had been applied for. This grant coupled, with the £40,000 that had already been raised, meant that the Trust was close to reaching its target. However, the Heritage Lottery Fund's decision had to remain secret until it was announced on 10 April as part of their next series of major grants.

When the news was finally announced nine days later it appeared that the Trust was nearly home and dry but there was no room for complacency. As part of the crisis over the future of the Fleet a large network of supporters had been built up and the Trust was keen to maintain contact with as many of these individuals as possible. It

111

To mark the 70th anniversary of the founding of Hunter's Fleet the Friends of the Hunter Fleet organised a major event at the Yard on 22 September 2001. Everyone was invited to dress up in 1930s style clothing for the event. The day began with the arrival of Cyril Hunter's daughter Jennifer Mack in Ron Bonshor's 1931 Talbot car.

© Celia and Fred Belbin

Sundew on the River Bure. © Richard Johnstone-Bryden

was decided that the most effective method of achieving this would be to form a friends organisation, so "The Friends Of The Hunter Fleet" was established in the summer of 1996. In addition to publishing a newsletter three times a year, to keep members informed of developments within the Fleet, the Friends provide on-going support for the Trust in two forms. Firstly, by providing volunteers to help out around the Yard. Secondly, with regular donations to purchase specific items. For example, in 2001 the Friends donated money to pay for new dinghy sails, exhibition boards and a camera to photograph the building of the new 4 berth yacht. The Friends also organise two social events at the Yard, which usually includes an opportunity to sail the boats. At the time of writing the membership has grown from 250 people in 1996 to over 700 and climbing.

After another successful season, in which bookings continued to rise, the Trust was able to formally complete the purchase of Hunter's Fleet on 30 September 1996. NCC's County Education Officer, Michael Edwards, acted as the Council's official representative for the short ceremony, which was concluded by the symbolic presentation of a County Sailing Base burgee to Michael Edwards. In many ways the event was something of an anticlimax because the Trust had been in control of the

Simon Crudgington at the helm of *Wood Avens*. Simon joined the Yard as an apprentice and learned to sail the yachts as part of his training.   © Richard Johnstone-Bryden

Fleet since April and there was not the same sense of anticipation as there had been at the earlier event. That said, it was still a significant milestone and it represented a major achievement for everyone who had been involved in the struggle to save the Yard.

Surprisingly, the purchase of the Fleet did not include the sale of the two half deckers *Brown Bess* and *Sundew*. The Council argued that neither boat was an integral part of the Fleet and that they had been specifically donated to the Council rather than the Yard. Therefore, they would retain ownership of both boats while the Trust would have the use of them and be responsible for their maintenance. Unconvinced by these arguments the Trust managed to make contact with the families that had originally donated each boat to see how they felt about the situation. Richard Sanders confirmed that he would like to see *Sundew* transferred to the Trust, as did Mrs Hudson who said that her late husband would have wanted *Brown Bess* to remain as part of Hunter's Fleet. The issue was finally resolved in 1999 when NCC agreed to transfer both *Sundew* and *Brown Bess* to NHFT.

In keeping with the Heri-

The team at Hunter's Yard in 1996 (clockwise from the centre) Lisa Morgan, Ian Grapes, Simon Crudgington, Bryan Read, Graham Cooper and Tom Grapes.   © Eastern Daily Press

tage part of the Trust's title the Trustees were keen to employ an apprentice, so that Graham Cooper, Tom Grapes and Ian Grapes could pass on the skills they had acquired through a lifetime of maintaining and building wooden boats. In many respects the employment of an apprentice by the Trust is a rather noble act because in today's world it is unrealistic to expect that someone who joins the Yard when they are 16 years old will still be there by the time they reach retirement age. So far the Trust's experience with apprentices reflect

this fact. Their first apprentice was Simon Crudgington who joined the Yard in 1996. During his five years with the Yard he showed great aptitude for boatbuilding and became a competent boatbuilder before his departure in 2001.

Another aspect of the Trust's title led to the first expansion of the Fleet since 1973 when *Rebel Reveller* was purchased in the Autumn of 1997. As part of the forward maintenance programme it was known that *Woodcut* would have to be withdrawn from the Fleet for a major restoration in either

Graham Cooper and Simon Crudgington fitting new timbers on-board *Rebel Reveller* during her restoration.

© Richard Johnstone-Bryden

1999, or 2000. The winter work load meant that this task could only be carried out during the summer months, but the Trust were keen to avoid the loss of any half decker capacity because they were proving to be an effective method of introducing new people to the Fleet. While the Trustees were considering what to do, Lisa Morgan discovered that Paul Williams wanted to sell *Rebel Reveller*. Lisa thought the idea of purchasing a Rebel would be a good solution to the *Woodcut* issue because it would fill the gap, left while she was being refitted, as well as introducing an example of another Broad-

land One Design Class to the Fleet. The Trustees backed this idea, not least because the Trust manages a Norfolk Heritage Fleet, so it is only right and proper that they should consider operating examples of different types of native Broadland sailing craft.

The gunter rigged Rebel One Design was designed by Alan Buchanan for the Horning based boatbuilders R Moore & Sons. Appropriately enough the first boat was built for Ralph Moore himself and named *Rebel*. Even though the attractive Rebels are exciting boats to sail, they were expensive to build compared to other Broad-

Rebel Reveller takes to the water following her restoration at the Yard on 25 September 1999. © Richard Johnstone-Bryden

land classes, such as the more numerous Yare & Bure One Design. This in turn restricted the development of the class, with only 13 Rebels being built between 1950 and 1962. However, if the experience of other Broadland One Design Classes are anything to go by, the Rebel may be set for a revival, following Colin Facey's decision to build a GRP version in 2004.

Rebel Reveller became the ninth Rebel to be completed, when she was launched as *Rebel Hood* in 1956. She was commissioned by H. Collins who sailed her until 1966, when she was purchased by I.D. Coutts, who renamed her *Rebel Reveller*. He sold her in 1982 to Andy Beardshaw, who in turn sold her to Gerald Thomas in 1988 before she changed hands again. Paul Williams bought her about two years later with the intention of restoring her himself. Sadly, he had never had the time to do the work himself so NHFT was able to pick up where he left off.

Rebel Reveller was moved into the boatshed once the rest of the Fleet had been launched for the 1998 hire season. As part of the work about 150ft of mahogany planking was replaced, and nearly all the 1 inch x 5/8 inch oak timbers

117

Rebel Reveller on the River Thurne on 25 September 1999. She is being sailed by (left to right) Paul Bowen, Martin Kirby, who as the Deputy Editor of the Eastern Daily Press helped to keep the media campaign going to save the Fleet, and Simon Crudgington.

© Richard Johnstone-Bryden

were renewed. Work resumed in the spring of 1999 after the winter break and included the fitting of a new 3/8 inch marine plywood deck, topped with West epoxy system. The seams were all recaulked and sika flexed to ensure that she remained bone dry when she was re-launched.

On completion of the restoration work she took to the water for the first time in nearly ten years on 25th September 1999. After about an hour she had been rigged and was ready for Tom Grapes to take the helm for her "maiden" sail. The sail plan of the Rebel was optimised for racing so it was de-

cided to curb her performance by chartering her with the smaller 70 sq ft jib. Even with this change, the Trust only hire her to experienced sailors who can fully appreciate her lively handling.

For the 2000 hire season the Trust operated all five of its half deckers, before *Woodcut* was withdrawn from service at the end of the season. Her restoration was not carried out as quickly as *Rebel Reveller's* because it coincided with the Yard's biggest project since 1949. As part of the Trust's initial objectives, there was a commitment to build a new yacht to one of the Hunter de

Graham Cooper at the helm of *Luna* on the River Thurne.

© Richard Johnstone-Bryden

designs. Originally, it was suggested that the construction of a new yacht would be an excellent way for the Trust to mark the Millennium, but the project remained on the back burner as the Trust dealt with more pressing issues. It was clear from the start of *Rebel Reveller's* restoration that a major boat building project was an effective method of generating continued interest in the work of the Yard, so Lisa Morgan decided to broach the subject with the Trustees during one of their regular committee meetings in June 1998. From customer feedback it was clearly evident that there would be most demand for another 4 berth yacht, so Graham Cooper prepared a rough estimate for the meeting. These figures showed that the

new yacht would cost £10,275 in materials and another £10,000 in labour. Following further discussions, the project was finally given the go-ahead in July 1999, but the issue of what to call the new yacht was left open and will not be settled until shortly before the launch, thus maintaining an element of mystery. To help raise money towards the construction costs the Trust introduced a targeted fund raising scheme whereby people could pay for specific items, such as the rudder, or the oil lamps. At the time of writing, £12,000 has been raised for the yacht.

Before work could begin on the new yacht there was the small issue of plans. None of the original Hunter drawings appeared to have survived, so

119

The new 4 berth yacht begins to take shape at the Yard during 2001. Her name will not be chosen by the Trust until shortly before her launch.

Both photographs © Richard Johnstone-Bryden

Graham Cooper quanting Luna.

Graham Cooper had to take the lines of *Luna* during the winter of 2000/2001 to produce a new set of plans. Although some of the original building moulds survived at the Yard, they were of little use until Graham could produce a new set of lines and incorporate them accordingly. The basic design for the 4 berth yachts has stood the test of time very well and there was little room for improvement, apart from the need to eliminate some minor weaknesses that have come to light over the years. One such area in need of improvement was the method of construction used for the bulkheads. In the earlier yachts traditional panelled bulkheads were installed, whereas today plywood is normally used as the core material, with the hardwood panelling providing additional strength.

Having obtained the measurements little further work was done until the spring of 2001, following the launch of the Fleet for the coming season. Once the boatshed had been cleared, some sheets of MDF were laid on the workshop floor and painted white. The measurements that Graham had taken were then "lofted out" (plotted) full size on to the MDF boards to produce the shape of the yacht. These lines where then faired to create the final shape of the hull. As part of this last process Graham raised the lines of the stern, to counter-act the inevitable drooping process that has gradually affected the 4 berth yachts as they get older. Once Graham was happy with the lines he was able to lay the keel of the new yacht in the "building berth" at the top of the oldest boatshed, where the majority of Hunter's Fleet was built. Like the restoration of *Rebel Reveller* the construction of the new yacht has had to take second place to the Fleet's maintenance work, so progress has been rather spasmodic and confined to the summer months. Interestingly, the selection of building materials proved surprisingly controversial. To ensure that the new yacht was accepted as a "proper" Hunter yacht Graham naturally decided that he would follow Percy Hunter's choice of mahogany planking on oak frames. After all, the idea of a painted yacht within Hunter's Fleet seems unthinkable. However, some members of the Friends strongly objected to the choice for environmental reasons, including the organisation's first Chairman, Richard

Ian Grapes works on *Woodcut*.
© Richard Johnstone-Bryden

Woodcut on the River Thurne.
© Richard Johnstone-Bryden

Sargant who resigned over the decision.

While work got underway on the new yacht, little progress was made with *Woodcut's* restoration, so Ian Grapes decided to take on the task as his first major project at the Yard. Although Graham has undertaken the lion share of the Yard's boatbuilding work, Ian trained as a boatbuilder before joining the Yard in 1981, so *Woodcut's* restoration gave him a rare opportunity to use his boatbuilding skills. By the time *Woodcut* was ready to rejoin the Fleet, in 2003, about the only original parts of her hull were the stem, hog and transom. Her return co-incided with the arrival of the gunter rigged Yare & Bure One Design (Y&BOD) *Buff Tip,* which has joined Hunter's Fleet on loan from the Gill family to increase the Fleet's range of half deckers. The Y&BOD was designed by the Norfolk boat-builder Ernest Woods in re-sponse to an invitation from the Yare & Bure Sailing Club in 1908 to produce a design to be raced by its members. The first Y&BODs were sold for £57 10s and the Class quickly grew in popularity, especially after the First World War when the Broadland yachting scene was dominated by small sailing boats, raced by amateur yachts-men. The early boats were all named after butterflies but, when the supply of names ran out, it was agreed to use the names of moths. The Y&BOD is now the biggest One Design Class on the Norfolk Broads. Like many of the other Broad-land One Designs the class is enjoying a period of expansion, thanks to the building of GRP Y&BODs by the Norwich based boatbuilder Kingsley Far-rington, who built the first GRP example in 1980. *Buff Tip* was launched in 1927 and she was the first Y&BOD to be built by Ernest Woods, following the

The Yare & Bure One Design *Buff Tip* joined the Fleet in 2003.
© Richard Johnstone-Bryden

movement of his business from Cantley to Horning. Although the Trust would like to incorpo-rate a few other Broadland sail-ing craft within the Fleet, the issue will require careful con-sideration, because space within the sheds is now at a premium during the winter months, thanks to the Trust's acquisitions since 1996.

Even though the major boatbuilding projects always attract people's attention they pale into insignificance com-pared to the mammoth task each winter of preparing the en-tire fleet for another hard sea-son of sailing. Since the Trust acquired the Fleet, the mainte-

Wood Anemone and the rest of the Fleet have been re-varnished and are nearly ready to be re-launched for another hard sailing season.

nance team have adhered to the proven routines, first established by Percy Hunter in the 1930s. As the season draws to a close each year, Graham and the team begin to plan the winter programme to ensure that they don't waste any time once the final hirers have completed their holidays. Inevitably, the boats will incur a certain amount of damage during the season. When accidents happen the damage is usually sorted out with a running repair, to keep the boat operational for the rest of the season, as well as ensuring that the hirer loses the minimum amount of time from their holiday. Where necessary, the work needed to complete a permanent repair will be incorpo-

rated into the winter programme. Over the years there has been a change in the type of accidents involving the Hunter boats. When the Hunters founded the Fleet the greatest cause of damage arose from collisions with other sailing craft, whereas encounters with quay heading now account for most of the damage incurred by the boats. This trend is explained by two factors. Firstly, the number of other sailing craft being sailed by inexperienced sailors has dramatically dropped, due to the decline in the numbers of sailing craft available for hire. Secondly, the amount of quay heading has steadily increased around the Broads since the 1930s. Before many of the river banks were piled, they consisted of reed banks which were very forgiving of hirers' mistakes. On those occasions, when a hirer ran out of water, they simply ploughed into the reed bank, denting their pride and not the boat, whereas a head on collision with solid quay heading nearly always inflicts serious damage to the boat. Equally, deteriorating quay heading is proving to be an increasing problem with its associated risks, such as submerged stakes that can rip open the hull below the waterline.

In reality permanent repairs to the season's damage only accounts for a small proportion of the winter schedule. The majority of the work carried out each winter is part of the long term maintenance programme for the Fleet. Wherever possible Graham and the team try to anticipate potential problems with the boats and take preventative measures, to ensure that each boat is kept to the high standards that people have come to expect of the Fleet. As the boats get older the scope of this programme will progressively increase. For example, some of the older boats have had to be re-planked above the waterline, as a direct result of repeated scrapping back to bare wood every ten to fifteen years which has worn down the thickness of the hull planks to the point where they are likely to be stove in by minor bumps incurred when coming alongside quay heading etc.

Obviously, it is not possible, or necessary, to strip all of the boats back to bare wood each winter, so the team focus their main efforts on one boat every winter, while conducting routine maintenance on the rest of the Fleet. The work on the boat selected for "intensive care" begins with the removal of the varnish to reveal all of the hull's blemishes, which are then eradicated either by routing out the damaged wood, or replacing an entire plank of wood. When all of the wood work is completed the stain can be applied. Sharp-eyed observers will have noticed that the colour of the yachts has slightly changed in recent years because the large stock of stain, built up by the Hunter family, has finally been exhausted and cannot be replaced because it is no longer in production. So far Tom Grapes and Graham Cooper have been unable to find a modern alternative to match the original colour. However, it is not a major problem as there

Above: *Wood Sorrel* on the River Thurne.

was always a slight difference in colour between the boats, because they were stained a much darker colour to allow for the progressive lightening effect caused by prolonged exposure to the sun during the summer months. Once the wood is the right colour, the process of applying the 7 coats of varnish begins. This may sound excessive but the high number of coats is necessary to keep out the weather and maintain a high standard of finish throughout the season. Even though the work is carried out inside the boatshed the prevailing weather conditions play a critical role while the boats are being varnished especially during the application of the final coats. If the atmosphere is too humid, or the temperature is too low, the varnish will not reach the "Hunter Standard".

Meanwhile, the work on the other boats is split into manageable chunks, beginning with the cabin tops, rails and blocks, followed by cabin sides, toe rails, and then the hull, before concluding with the application of the white line and the anti foul. The logic behind this approach is that all of the muck and debris flows downwards. All of the boats are worked on in the same order, so when they varnish the cabin sides it is not only one boat that has to be done, but thirteen! Just as in the days of the Hunter family, each member of the team concentrates upon their area of expertise, with Ian Grapes working on the high level tasks (cabin tops, cabin sides and cockpit wells) Tom Grapes does the hulls, while Graham Cooper carries out the wood work. Providing all is well, the high level work is finished by Christmas and the hulls are on their way. Every year Graham and Tom think they are running out of time, but somehow the team always manages to get the Fleet back in the water for Easter. Despite the comprehensive nature of the winter maintenance programme there never seems to be enough time to do much work on the interiors. When the Hunter family owned the Yard they would carry out some re-varnishing work on a yacht's interior during the summer, if it was not out on hire for a week or so. Today, the Trust can not afford to do this, in case someone rings up wanting to book a yacht at short notice, so the team do what they can, either at the beginning, or end of the season.

Of course none of this work would be possible without

the skilled team of craftsmen who maintain the Fleet. However, it is this aspect of maintaining the boats that could pose the greatest challenge for the Trust during the 21st Century. The Fleet has been extremely fortunate in that there has been a very low turnover of staff during the past 50 years. At the time of writing the core maintenance team consists of Graham Cooper, Tom Grapes and Ian Grapes, who between them have over 100 years experience of working on these fine vessels. Inevitably, there will come a time when they will want to retire. Finding their successors is going to be a very difficult task. Ideally, the Trust needs to attract boatbuilders who are young enough to work at the Yard for at least 15 - 20 years, so that they will be able to learn all of the quirks of the boats and have the time to be able to train their successors. Without this level of continuity, there is the very real risk that it will not be possible to keep the boats in the manner we have all come to expect, and this would be a tragedy. After all, it looks as though there is no shortage of people wanting to experience the thrill of sailing a Hunter boat. As people's leisure time continues to increase there is a growing number of people who hire a Hunter boat as their second or third holiday. Equally, the Fleet has also benefited in recent years from the developing short break market.

It is remarkable that Hunter's Fleet has managed to survive unscathed through such troubled waters. As the oldest boats begin their eighth decade it will be interesting to see how the Fleet continues to develop under the guidance of the Trust which has already proved, through its achievements to date, that it has the financial ability to fund the work needed to keep both the Yard and the boats up to the "Hunter Standard" as required. Inevitably, when one writes about an ongoing story, the author is always left with questions about the future. Will the 4 berth yacht be the last such boat to be built at the Yard? Will the Fleet acquire examples of other types of Broadland half deckers? And will Woodruff ever rejoin the Fleet? Only time will tell but the outlook for this unique Broadland fleet has never looked as good as it does today so let us hope it stays that way.

Getting away from it all with Hunter's Fleet.

©Richard Johnstone-Bryden

Cyril Hunter at the helm of his favourite boat within the fleet, *Hustler 2*, near Thurne Mouth.

Appendix I

The Details

In preparing this section it was discovered that some of the yachts differed from the measurements previously used in various brochures since the Fleet first appeared in the Blakes brochure in 1932. In the interests of accuracy Graham Cooper and Ian Grapes measured each of the boats in January 2004 to determine the exact measurements for this section of the book.

Percy Hunter with some of the tenders at the Yard.

(via Jim Searle)

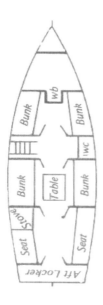 

Lustre Class

Origin of Name:	The first two letters for each name are LU for Ludham
Completed:	*Lustre* 1932
	Lullaby 1932
	Luna 1933
	Keel laid of 4th yacht April 2001 (name to be announced at the launching ceremony)
Length:	*Lustre* 28ft 8ins
	Lullaby 28ft 5ins
	Luna 28ft 8ins
	The new yacht 29ft 2ins
Beam:	8ft 6ins
Draft:	2ft 6ins
Sail Area:	Main Sail 378 sq ft
	Jib 50 sq ft
No. of Berths:	4
Headroom:	5ft 9ins (Measured at the highest point with the cabin top raised)

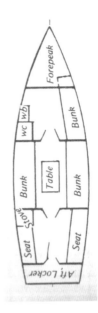

Wood Class

Origin of Name: The first two letters of each name are WO for Womack Water and each yacht is named after a type of flower.

Completed: *Woodruff* 1932 (Sold off 1973)
Wood Sorrel 1933
Wood Violet 1934
Wood Rose 1935
Wood Avens 1947
Wood Anemone 1949 (built for £313)

Length: *Wood Sorrel* 23ft 10ins
Wood Violet 24ft
Wood Rose 23ft 10ins
Wood Avens 23ft 10ins
Wood Anemone 24ft

Beam: 7ft 6ins
Draft: 2ft 6ins
Sail Area: Main Sail 268 sq ft
Jib 34 sq ft
No. of Berths: 3
Headroom: 5ft 9in (Measured at the highest point with the cabin top raised)

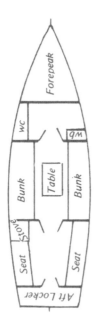

Hustler Class

Origin of Name:	The first two letters of each name are HU for Hunter
Completed:	*Hustler* 1936
	Hustler 2 1936
	Hustler 3 1937
	Hustler 4 1938
	Hustler 5 1939
Length:	*Hustler* 24ft 4ins
	Hustler 2 24ft 3ins
	Hustler 3 24ft 3ins
	Hustler 4 24ft 4ins
	Hustler 5 24ft 5ins
Beam:	7ft 6ins
Draft:	2ft 6ins
Sail Area:	Main sail 286 sq ft
	Jib 57 sq ft
Number of Berths:	2
Headroom:	5ft 9ins (Measured at the highest point with the cabin top raised)

Woodcut Class

Origin of Name: To determine the origin of the name it should be split into two sections to gain the most likely explanation. The first half of the name was possibly an extension of the Womack Water theme used for the Wood Class yachts while the second half of the name might have been inspired by the dyke which the Hunters often referred to as "The Cut"

Completed:	*Woodcut*	1933
	Woodcut II	1938
Length:	*Woodcut*	18ft 10ins
	Woodcut II	19ft 2ins
Beam:	6ft 2ins	
Draft:	2ft 6ins	
Sail Area:	190 sq ft	

Above: *Brown Bess.* © Richard Johnstone-Bryden

Middle Nene One Design

Name:	*Brown Bess*
Builder:	Percival, Horning
Introduced To Hunter's Fleet:	1968
Reconstructed:	1986 - 1987
Length:	20ft 2ins
Beam:	6ft 3ins
Draft:	2ft 6ins
Sail Area:	190 sq ft

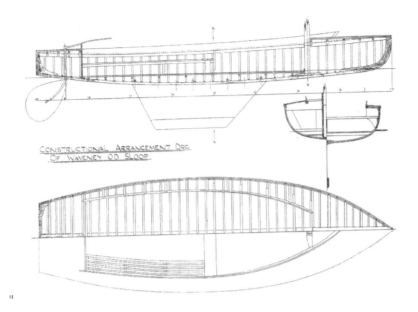

Above: Drawing courtesy of the Waveney One Design Class

Waveney One Design

Origin of Name:	The Waveney One Designs were all named after wild plants or flowers growing on the marshes
Name:	*Sundew*
Designer:	W.J. Parker
Builder:	Jack Fowler
Completed:	1951
Class Number:	18
Introduced To Hunter's Fleet:	1973
Length:	22ft 3 1/2in
Beam:	6ft
Draft:	2ft 9in
Sail Area:	Main Sail 230.5 sq ft
	Jib 59.5 sq ft

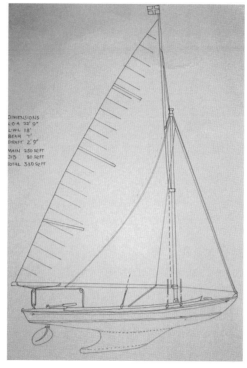

DIMENSIONS
LOA 22' 9"
LWL 18'
BEAM 7'
DRAFT 2' 9"

MAIN 250 SQ FT
JIB 80 SQ FT
TOTAL 330 SQ FT

Above: Photograph of drawing of Rebel OD by Alex Humphris

Rebel One Design

Name:	*Rebel Reveller*
Designer:	Alan Buchanan
Builder:	R Moore & Sons
Completed:	1956
Class Number:	9
Introduced To Hunter's Fleet:	1999
Length Overall:	22ft 9ins
Length Water Line:	18ft
Beam:	7ft
Draft:	3ft
Sail Area:	Mainsail 278 sq ft
	Racing Jib 80 sq ft
	Cruising Jib 70 sq ft (This is the size jib used for Rebel Reveller)

Above: Drawing of Y&BOD reproduced courtesy of the Yare &
          Bure One Design Class

Yare & Bure One Design

Origin of Name: The Yare & Bure One Designs
                                       were all named after butterflies
                                       and when the supply of names
                                       ran out the Class allowed   the
                                       use of moth names.

Name: *Buff Tip*
Designer: Ernest Woods
Builder: Ernest Woods
Completed: 1927
Class Number: 34
Introduced To Hunter's Fleet: 2003
Length Overall: 20ft
Length Water Line: 18ft
Beam: 6ft
Draft: 2ft 9ins
Sail Area: Mainsail 217 sq ft
                                       Jib 58 sq ft

Top: A rare photograph of *Saskia*. (via Jim Searle)

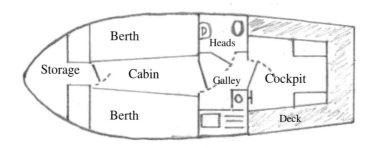

Motor Cruiser *Saskia*

Introduced To Hunter's Fleet:	1962
Sold off	1977
Completed:	Early 1950s
Builder:	Collins Pleasurecraft, Oulton Broad
Length:	22ft
Beam:	8ft
Engine:	4 cylinder Morris Vedette 8HP
Top Speed:	6 Knots
Number of Berths:	2
Headroom:	6ft

Appendix II

Notable Events

I have tried to provide exact dates wherever possible but unfortunately the available information for some of the events listed below can only confirm in which year the particular event occurred.

1932
- 6 February, Percy Hunter purchased the land for Hunter's Yard.
- The dyke linking Womack Water and the site of the proposed boat sheds is excavated.
- *Lullaby* and *Lustre* are launched.
- *Woodruff* is built by Alfred Pegg at Wroxham.
- Hunter's Fleet is listed within the annual Blakes brochure for the first time.

1933
- 2 August, Smallburgh Rural District Council granted planning permission for the construction of the first shed at Ludham.
- *Luna*, *Wood Sorrel* and *Woodcut* are launched.

1934
- *Wood Violet* is launched.

1935
- *Wood Rose* is launched.
- 3 July, Smallburgh Rural District Council granted planning permission for the construction of the second boat shed.

1936
- *Hustler* and *Hustler 2* are launched.

1937
- *Hustler 3* is launched.

1938
- *Hustler 4* and *Woodcut 2* are launched.

1939
- *Hustler 5* is launched.
- August, anticipating the outbreak of WWII Percy ends the hire season early to enable him to slip the Fleet before they are requi-

sitioned by the Government.

1944

- The Government granted permission for Percy Hunter & Sons to re-launch the Fleet and resume the hiring out of their boats.

1947

- *Wood Avens* is launched.

1949

- *Wood Anemone* is built for £313 1s 5d.

1951

- 14 November, Percy Hunter & Sons formally becomes a Company Limited by Shares.

1952

- *Hustler 2* became the first yacht within the fleet to exchange her cotton sails for Terylene sails. Nylon ropes are also introduced to replace the manila and hemp ropes.

1956

- The primus stoves are replaced by gas stoves onboard the Wood and Lustre Classes.

1960

- The primus stoves are replaced by gas stoves onboard the Hustlers.

1962

- The 22ft motor cruiser *Saskia* joins Hunter's Fleet.

1964

- 26 January, Percy Hunter dies.

1967

- 9 September, Norfolk Education Committee recommends the purchase of Hunter's Yard by Norfolk County Council.
- 7 October, Norfolk County Council agrees to purchase Hunter's Fleet by a 15 vote majority.

1968

- 1 January, Norfolk County Council purchase Hunter's Fleet and renames the yard Norfolk County Sailing Base.
- Stanley Hunter retires.
- Dr Hudson donates the Middle Nene One Design *Brown Bess* to Hunter's Fleet.
- Hunter's Fleet are listed within the Blakes brochure for the last time.

1969

- The Norfolk Wherry Trust is granted permission to moor their trading wherry *Lord Roberts* in the basin at the top of the dyke .

1973

- The Waveney One Design *Sundew* is donated to Hunter's Fleet by Richard Sanders.
- *Woodruff* is written off by a major gas explosion and subsequently sold.

1974

- *Lord Roberts* is raised but soon sinks again.
- Cyril Hunter retires.

1977

- The 22ft Motor Cruiser *Saskia* is sold off.

1978

- Graham Cooper builds the Bass Boat.

1982

- Speculation in the press about the future of Hunter's Fleet as a result of Norfolk County Council's review of extra curricular facilities. The Fleet is subsequently retained and How Hill is sold instead.

1983

- Hunter's Yard and *Lullaby* are used by the BBC in their production of Arthur Ransome's stories Coot Club and Big Six.
- *Lord Roberts* is raised again and towed to private moorings in Hoveton where she subsequently sank again.

1988

- May, The new *Brown Bess* is launched by Dr Hudson.

1995

- 18 January, The Education Committee agrees to explore the option of selling the Norfolk County Sailing Base.
- 23 February, Norfolk County Council's decision to sell Hunter's Fleet becomes front page news of the Eastern Daily Press sparking an immediate public outcry.
- 1 March, Eastern Daily Press launches its "Save Our Sailfleet" Campaign.
- 1 March, The Norfolk Heritage Fleet Steering Group meets for the first time.

8 June, The bids for Hunter's Fleet are reviewed by Norfolk

County Council's Education Committee to produce a short list of two organisations for the final round of negotiations. Norfolk Broads Yachting Co steps aside in favour of the Norfolk Heritage Fleet Trust leaving the Trust as the sole bidder.

- 16 August, Norfolk County Council announce their agreement in principle to sell Hunter's Fleet to the Trust.

1996

- 1 April, Norfolk Heritage Fleet Trust takes on responsibility for Hunter's Fleet and Paul Heiney launches the public appeal to raise £300,000 to purchase the Fleet.
- 10 April, The Heritage Lottery Fund awards a grant of £200,000 towards the purchase of Hunter's Fleet.
- 1 August, raffle of David Dane's oil painting The First Sail Of The Day to raise funds for the Trust.
- 30 September, Norfolk Heritage Fleet Trust completes the purchase of Hunter's Fleet. *Sundew* and *Brown Bess* remained the property of Norfolk County Council because the Council maintained that they had been donated to the Council and not the Fleet.

1997

- 26 April, inaugural general meeting of The Friends Of The Hunter Fleet.
- Summer, Concreting the floor of the second boatshed.
- Autumn, The Trust purchases *Rebel Reveller* for the Fleet.

1999

- *Sundew* and *Brown Bess* are formally transferred to Norfolk Heritage Fleet Trust from Norfolk County Council.
- 25 September, *Rebel Reveller* is re-launched and joins Hunter's Fleet following her £5000 restoration.

2000

- Boatshed roofs replaced at a cost of £28,000.

2001

- Work begins on the new 4 berth yacht.

2002

- Summer, Completion of south bank piling at a cost of £2,500.

2003

- *Woodcut* is re-launched following her restoration.
- The Yare & Bure One Design *Buff Tip* joins Hunter's Fleet.

Appendix III

Trustees of the Norfolk Heritage Fleet Trust

Left: *Hustler 2*,
May 1958

Both photographs via
Jennifer Mack

Below: Getting ready
for Easter

Appendix IV

Slipping The Fleet

Every year the hire season comes to an end when the final hirers leave the Yard during the first week of October. The following Monday morning the maintenance team begin the two week long task of preparing the Fleet for slipping. The range of tasks carried out for each boat during this period includes the removal of the awning, rigging, sails, bedding, mattresses, cooker, crockery and the mast. Once ashore these items are cleaned before being packed away for the winter months. All of the loose boards are then removed prior to the cleaning of the bilges and cab-

ins. Externally, the cabin sides and cockpit wells are rubbed down with pumice powder before the loose boards are put back onboard prior to slipping. Once all of this work is completed the two day process of hauling the Fleet out of the water can begin.

In the interests of safety the number of people present in the Yard during this operation is always kept to the essential members of the team. All other visitors are kept well away from the working area so very few people actually get to see this part of the Yard's work.

All photographs in Appendix IV
©Richard Johnstone-Bryden

The boats are now de-stored and await their turn to be slipped and moved into their position within the shed for the winter months.

Above: Darryl Jay (left) and Duncan Broadhurst prepare the slider in the greased wooden way. When the boat is in position the keel will sit on the slider. The safety stools can be seen in the background and are in position in case the recovery team lose control of the boat and it falls over.

Below: Duncan Broadhurst inserts the wedge which will hold the slider in position until the boat is manoeuvred into position and its weight is placed on the slider.

The greased way is now ready to receive the boat. The plank mounted on each side of the greased way will act as the guide to ensure the boat is centred on the greased way.

Wood Violet is guided into position for slipping

149

Above: Graham Cooper attaches the wire strop to the eye underneath the stem on to which the wire will be attached

Left: Lining up *Wood Violet* so that the greased way can be pushed under the boat

Above: Duncan Broadhurst lifts the greased way to push it under the boat

Below: *Wood Violet* is pulled up the greased way in preparation for attaching the winch wire

Above: The winch wire has been attached to the eye beneath the stem and *Wood Violet* is being pulled out of the water by the winch. The power of the winch is controlled by Graham Cooper using the yellow box in his hand which is connected to the winch by a long lead.

Below: Graham controls the speed at which *Wood Violet* is hauled out of the water and as she emerges from the water he physically balances her to keep her upright.

Wood Violet is edged towards the holding position at the entrance to the shed where she will be cleaned below the waterline.

The recovery team swarm around *Hustler 2* to complete the final stage of the pre-refit cleaning work. The anti foul is cleaned with the pressure washer and the brush while the white boot top is rubbed down with pumice powder. Effective team work enables this stage to be completed in a matter of moments. When this work is finished *Hustler 2* is moved inside the shed using a number of greased ways until she reaches her allocated winter berth.

Glossary & Abbreviations

Bilges The bilge is the bottom part of the hull either side of the keel which meets the sides. In most types of vessel the bilge meets the side in a curve and this part of the hull is known as the turn of the bilge

Blakes Letting agency founded by Henry Blake in 1908

Bow The foremost end of a boat / ship

Bowsprit The spar projecting over the bow from which a jib can be set

Broads Authority The Broads Authority is a Special Statutory Authority created by the Norfolk & Suffolk Broads Act 1988. The Act made the Broads Authority responsible for managing the Broads for the purposes of protecting the interests of navigation, conserving and enhancing the natural beauty of the Broads as well as promoting the enjoyment of the Broads by the public

Bulkheads A vertical partition dividing a boat into compartments

Carvel Construction Used to describe the hull of a boat with flush mounted planks as opposed to the overlapping planks of clinker construction

Coaster Small cargo ship or tanker moving cargoes in coastal waters between ports.

Dinghy From the Hindi word dengi or dingi. This term was originally used to describe a small open rowing boat used on rivers powered by one pair of oars and employed as a work boat in warships, merchant ships or as a tender to a yacht. After WWI dinghy racing became a major sport with the introduction of the International 14ft and National 12ft classes. Today there are several hundred classes of racing dinghies campaigned around the world.

Dory Most recently this term has been applied to a type of hard chine GRP dinghy powered by an outboard and used as either a rescue boat by a sailing club or as a tender

Dyke Normally used to describe a channel cut to drain marshes

EDP Eastern Daily Press

Fender Object used to protect the hull from bumps and chaffing while moored alongside. Fenders come in all shapes and sizes and are now normally made of some form of plastic.

GRP Glass-reinforced plastic

Half Decker Keel boats with a deck that covers only part of the hull

HDML Harbour Defence Motor Launch

Heads The name given to the part of the older sailing ships forward of the forecastle and around the bow used by the crew as their lavatory and used today to describe a marine lavatory. It was used in plural to indicate the weather and lee sides, seamen being expected to use the lee side so that all effluent should fall clear into the sea

Jib The triangular sail set forward of the mast. The self tacking jibs fitted to the Hunter yachts have a boom attached to the bottom edge of the sail. A loose footed jib has no boom along its bottom edge

Keel The lowest and principal timber of a wooden boat

Main Sail The principal sail

Mainsheet The rope used to control the position of the principal sail

MDF Medium Density Board manufactured by pressing wood fibre and resin

MTB Motor Torpedo Boat

Navigation Post Wooden posts used to mark a deep water channel

NBYCo Norfolk Broads Yachting Company

NCC Norfolk County Council

NHFT Norfolk Heritage Fleet Trust

Piling Vertical timber or metal protecting a river bank from erosion or to provide a stable banks for mooring

PR Public Relations

Punt 1 A small flat bottomed craft built in the form of a floating platform or stage.

2 A Norfolk Punt was defined in 1926 by the Norfolk Punt Club as "a strongly-built light draught open or partly decked wooden craft with pointed stem and stern, very low freeboard and nearly flat bottom, suited to the purpose of being quanted, rowed or sailed to fowl". The first Norfolk Punts appeared on Breydon water at the end of the 19th century and were fitted with a gun on the foredeck to shoot wildfowl. Some of the early gun punts used a small sprit sail as an alternative to rowing for getting across Breydon Water quickly. Punts were later developed purely for sailing with a balanced lugsail rig. The lugsail rig soon gave way to a sliding gunter rig with headsail before the Norfolk Punt Club allowed the use of any rig in 1933

Quant A wooden pole used to propel a boat

Sheerline The upward curve of the deck towards the bow and stern

Slipping / Slipped Bringing a boat ashore

Slipway An inclined plane or ramp on the shore extending into the water used to either launch boats or recover them from the water

Staithe A parish quay, originally used for loading or unloading cargo. Many staithes are now used for the mooring of boats including short term public mooring of boats

Stern The back end of a boat / ship

Tabernacle The wooden structure in which the mast is mounted on all Broads yachts. The forward section of the structure is open to enable the bottom of the mast to swing forward as the mast is lowered. The mast pivots on a bolt which passes through the top of the tabernacle

Timbers The frames or ribs of a wooden boat which provide the hull with both its shape and strength

Topping Lift The rope used to raise or lower the boom and to support the boom when the sail is lowered.

Transom stern A flat stern

Y&BOD Yare & Bure One Design

WOD Waveney One Design

Bibliography

During the course of my research for this book I have consulted the following published documents.

Various editions of:
Hunter's Yard - Newsletter of the Friends of the Hunter Fleet, the Hunter's Fleet Brochure,
Eastern Daily Press,
The Green Book (published annually by the Norfolk & Suffolk Yachting Association)
Classic Boat, and
The Blakes Brochure.

Waveney One Designs, by Charles George, Private Circulation

The Rebel One Design - A History And Reflections Of The Boats And Their Owners, by Alex Humphris, Private Circulation

More Memories From The Marshes - People Of The Broads Past And Present, by Margaret Dye, Larks Press, 1996

Boatman Of Broadland, by Margaret Dye, Larks Press, 1999

Broadland Sport, by Nicholas Everitt, Halsgrove, 2002

Hathor - The Story Of A Norfolk Pleasure Wherry, by Peter Bower, Broads Authority, 1989

The Man Who Found The Broads - A biography of George Christopher Davies, by Jamie Campbell & Cliff Middleton, Hamilton Publications Ltd, 1999

Hamilton's Navigations - The Definitive Guide To The Norfolk & Suffolk Broads, Edited by Jamie Campbell, 1997 and 2001 editions

Herbert Woods - A Famous Broadland Pioneer, by Jennifer Woods, Captains Locker Publications, 2002

Broads Plan 1997, Broads Authority, 1997

Still Waters, by Miles Hedley, Maas Books, 1999

Classic One Designs, by Jack Coote, Waterline Books, 1994

Arthur Ransome And The World Of The Swallows & Amazons, by Roger Wardale, Great Northern Books, 2000

Oxford Companion to Ships and the Sea, edited by Peter Kemp, Paladin Books, 1979

Index

A47 Road Bridge, 19
Acle, 20 40 75 90
Adcock, Mr, 67
Albion, 84
Ant, River, 17 25 76
Applegate, George, 43-5, 47 49 51 55

Bagnall-Oakley, Dick, 83
Barnes, Mike,108-9
Barton Broad, 25, 76
Bass Boat, 91
BBC, 93-4, 98
Beardshaw, Andy, 117
Beccles, 38
Beccles Amateur Sailing Club, 39
Berney Arms Public House, 31
Bitter Boys, 81-2
Black Horse Broad,26-7 44
Blackheath, 29
Blakes, 45 50 52 59 66-7 70
Boardman, Edward, 75-6
Boardman, Florence, 75
Bonshor, Lesley, 90
Bonshor, Ron, 90
Bower, Peter, 88
Breydon Regatta, 39
Breydon Water, 16 31 35 39 69 98
Broads Authority, 25 28 83 93 105
Brown, Colin, 92
Brown, Jimmy, 23
Brown Bess, 82-3 99 114
Buchanan, Alan, 116
Buckenham Ferry, 34 39
Brundall, 34-5
Buff Tip, 123
Bure, River, 17 19 20-1 24-6 28 75
Burgh Castle, 35

Candle Dyke, 23
Cantley, 34 44 123
Chedgrave, 34
Chet, River, 29 34
Clark, Professor Aitken, 105
Clayton, Professor Keith, 105
Coldham Hall Public House, 35 39
Coldham Sailing Club, 39
Cole, John, 82

Colins Pleasure Craft, 71
Collins, H, 117
Coltishall, 28
Cooper, Candy, 109
Cooper, Graham, 87 91 99 103 109 115
119 121-2 124-5 127-8
Coutts, I.D., 117
Crudgington, Simon, 115

Dale, Dikky, 81
de Carl Smith, Mr, 71
de longh, Basil, 105
Death & Glory, 94
Driscoll, John, 92

Eastern Daily Press, 103-4 106 109
Edwards, Michael, 104-5 113

Facey, Colin, 117
Farrington, Kingsley, 123
Filby Broad, 74
Filby Sailing Base, 74 78 91
Fleet Dyke, 24
Fowler, Jack, 88
Friends Of The Hunter Fleet, 113

Gaviota, 75
Gee, Les, 74 78 84 87
Geldeston Lock, 38
Grapes, Ian, 94 99 103 115 122 127-8
Grapes, Tom, 66-7 69 78 99 103 115 118
125 127-8
Great Yarmouth, 19 20 22 29 31
Great Yarmouth Fire Brigade, 84
Great Yarmouth Port and Haven Commis-
sion, 91 105
Green, Charles, 44 47

Haddiscoe Bridge, 36
Heigham Sound, 23
Heiney, Paul, 110
Henderson, F, 88
Heritage Yacht Fleet Trust, 104
Hickling Broad, 23
Hornor, Sam, 105
Horning, 17 22 24 26-7 40 83 123
Horning Sailing Club, 41

Horsey Mere, 17, 23-4
Hoveton Great Broad, 27
How Hill, 75-6 93
Hudson, Dr Harold, 77 82 99
Hudson, Mrs, 114
Hunter, Cyril, 43-5 47 49 54 59 60 62 65 67-70 73 78 83 98
Hunter,(now Witton) Elizabeth, 69
Hunter, Ethel, 54
Hunter, Harry, 47
Hunter (now Mack), Jennifer, 65
Hunter, Michael, 65
Hunter, Muriel, 67
Hunter, Percy, 43-5 47 49-51 54-5 58-63 65 68 70-1 73 121 124
Hunter, Phyllis, 54
Hunter, Stanley, 43-5 47 49 54-5 62 65 67-70 73 78
Hustler Class 58-9 81
Hustler 2, 81
Hustler 5, 59

John Henry, 75-6

Kirby, Martin, 106
Kittywake, 81

Langley Staithe, 34
Loddon, 34
Lord Roberts, 83-4
Lowestoft, 29 36
Ludham, 15 22 25 44 47 54 59 60 62 70 78 83 91 93 104
Ludham Fire Brigade, 62 67
Lullaby, 47 50 93-4 98
Luna, 55 121
Lustre, 47 50

Malthouse Broad, 25
Margoletta, 98
Martham Boatbuilding & Development Co, 23
Martham Broad, 23
Martham Ferry, 23
May Gurney, 84
McCully, Miss, 78
Meadow Dyke, 23
Middle Nene One Design, 83
Middle Nene Sailing Club, 83
Mogford, Leslie, 105
Moore, Ralph, 116

Morgan, Lisa, 103 105 109 116 119
Museum of the Broads, 25 83-4

National Heritage Lottery Fund, 109 111
New Cut, 36
Nicholas Everitt Park, 38
Norfolk Broads Yacht Club, 27 40
Norfolk Broads Yachting Co, 108-9
Norfolk County Council, 74 77 80-2 84 87-8 94 99 106 109 114
Norfolk County Council, Education Authority, 75-7 87 93 105
Norfolk County Council, Education Committee, 76 91 101 103 104 108
Norfolk County Council, Planning Department, 75 84
Norfolk County Sailing Base, 78 88 91 98 110 113
Norfolk Heritage Fleet Steering Group, 105-9
Norfolk Heritage Fleet Trust 109-11 113-4 116-9 123 127-8
Norfolk Property Services, 103 105 107
Norfolk Schools Sailing Association, 92
Norfolk Wherry Trust, 84
Norfolk Windmill Trust, 20
Norwich, 29 35-6
Norwich Union, 93
Nudd, Roger, 78

Olive, 87-8
Oulton Broad, 38-9 71 84
Oulton Dyke, 36
Oulton Week, 38

Parker, William, 88
Pegg, Alfred, 51-2
Percivals, 83
Pitt Steele, Mr C.A., 76-7
Pleasure Boat Public House, 23 82
Potter Heigham, 22 40 44-5 62-3 82 98
Priscilla, 71

Ralphs, Dr Lincoln, 74-6 91
Ransome, Arthur, 93
Ranworth, 25
Read, Bryan, 105, 111
Rebel One Design, 41, 116
Rebel Reveller (Rebel Hood), 115-9 121
Reedham, 31 34
Reedham Ferry, 31 39

Reedling One Design, 41
Richardson, Patrick, 22
Richardson, Robin, 22
Roberts, Ken, 81
Rockland Broad, 34
Rodley & Co, 98
Roualle, Frances, 91-2

St Benet's Abbey, 24
St Olaves, 35-6
Salhouse, 27
Sanders, Richard, 88 114
Sanders, W, 88
Sargant, Richard, 122
Saskia, 71 87
Scouts, 82
Scripture Union, 82
Searle, Jim, 87 91 99
Smallburgh Rural District Council, 47
Somerleyton, 36 38
South Walsham, 24 55
Southgate Dick, 74
Southgate, George, 74
Stalham, 25
Stalham Fire Brigade, 84
Stevens, Paul, 105
Stokesby, 20 75
Stracey Arms, 20
Sundew, 88 114
Sunrise, 55
Sunset, 55
Surlingham Broad, 35
Sutton Broad, 25

Taylor, Reggie, 60
Taylor's of Wroxham, 59
Teasel, 93-4 98
Thatcher, Margaret, 91
Thomas, Gerald, 117
Thurne, River, 17, 21-2 24-5 55 70
Thurne Dyke, 22
Thurne Mouth, 20 41
Thrower, Pat, 47
Titmouse, 94 98
Trafford, Anthony, 105
Turner, Dr George, 102-3 105

Upton, 21

Vauxhall Bridge, 19

Wannick, 70
Waveney, River, 29 35-6 38
Waveney & Oulton Broad Sailing Club, 39
Waveney One Design, 39 88
Waveney Sailing Club, 88
Wayford, 25
Webb, Christopher, 92
Webb, Josie, 78 103
Wensum, River, 29 35
West Somerton, 23
Williams, Paul, 116
Womack Staithe, 22 44
Womack Water, 22 25 44-6
Wind Rush, 67
Wood Avens, 66-7 69 70
Wood Anemone, 66-7 70
Wood Rose, 58
Wood Sorrel, 55
Wood Violet, 58
Woodruff, 51-2 88 90
Woods, Ernest, 67 123
Woods, Herbert, 22 26-7 62
Woodcut, 55 70 115-6 118 122
Woodcut 2, 60
Wroxham, 24 27-8 40 54

Yare, River, 29 34-6
Yare & Bure One Design, 41 67 88 117 123
Yare Navigation Race, 39
Yare Sailing Club, 39